SEASONAL PLANTING GUIDE AND CALENDAR

FOR SOUTH CAROLINA SCHOOL AND COMMUNITY GARDENS

CREATED AND WRITTEN BY:
AMY L. DABBS, School and Community Gardening Coordinator, Clemson Extension and
ZACHARY SNIPES, Commercial Horticulture Agent, Clemson Extension

CONTENT SPECIALISTS:
Justin Ballew, Robert Last, S. Cory Tanner, Patricia Whitener and Stephanie Turner

BOOK DESIGN BY:
Torborg Davern Design

REVIEWED BY:
Thomas Litton, Janet Litton and Dawn Anticole White

CONTENTS

WELCOME	1
SCHOOL GARDEN CHECKLIST AND WORKSHEET	2
COMMUNITY GARDEN CHECKLIST AND WORKSHEET	6
RAISED BED GARDENING	10
SHEET COMPOSTING AND WATERING	11
SEASONAL CLASSIFICATION OF VEGETABLE CROPS	12
PLANT FAMILIES	13
FRUIT IN THE GARDEN	14
HERBS IN THE GARDEN	15
MANAGING PESTS IN SCHOOL AND COMMUNITY GARDENS	16
POLLINATORS AND BENEFICIAL INSECTS	18
COMMON PESTS OF VEGETABLE CROPS	20
COMMON DISEASES OF VEGETABLE CROPS	21
FOOD SAFETY, HARVESTING AND STORAGE	22
SCHOOL AND COMMUNITY GARDENS PLANTING GUIDE	25
RECOMMENDED PLANTING PLAN AND CALENDAR FOR SCHOOL GARDENS	26
PLANNING A YEAR-ROUND SCHOOL OR COMMUNITY GARDEN	42
CROP PROFILES FOR SCHOOL AND COMMUNITY GARDENS	45
TEMPLATES	51
ENDNOTES	58

WELCOME
TO SCHOOL & COMMUNITY GARDENING

On behalf of Clemson Extension, we would like to thank you for planting the first seed for your school or community garden. When people gather to cultivate a vegetable garden, incredible things happen. Gardens increase access to fresh, nutritious food and help people develop healthy eating habits. Young people learn essential life skills, and as a result, communities become stronger.

Since 2012, Clemson Extension has led the way in a growing school gardening movement across our state. We began by developing School Gardening for SC Educators, a comprehensive horticulture-based training and technical support program that helps schools establish and maintain sustainable, edible school gardens. Since then, we have worked with nearly two thousand educators, community gardeners, partnering agencies, and volunteers to establish hundreds of gardens statewide. This technical guide has been a critical element of the program's success, but it needed to be updated to reflect our clients' emerging needs better.

The Seasonal Planting Guide & Calendar for South Carolina School and Community Gardens includes a community gardening guide, crop profiles, common insect pests, diseases of vegetables, and a harvesting guide. School gardeners will find sample planting plans and calendars to follow throughout the school year for maximum vegetable yields. Community gardeners will find a helpful checklist and expanded planting plans for year-round vegetable gardening options.

We hope you will connect with your local Clemson Extension office to discover the network of resources available to support your community-based gardening project!

Your friends in the garden,

The Clemson Extension School & Community Gardening Team

Charping, L. Clemson University

SCHOOL GARDEN
CHECKLIST & WORKSHEET

☐ BUILD A TEAM

When a team of educators, school staff, administrators, parents, and volunteers come together with students to build a school garden, the results are successful, sustainable outdoor classrooms. Begin by building a core team willing to learn and work alongside you. Who is on your team? List them here:

☐ ENGAGE ADMINISTRATORS

School administrators are crucial to giving your school gardening team the time and space you will need to organize, implement, and grow a school garden. Supportive school administrators can help overcome parent and staff objections and advocate on your behalf with maintenance personnel and district-level staff. Don't stop with school administrators; communicate garden plans with members of parent-teacher-student groups and other community stakeholders to gain support for your school garden program.

⟫ ACTION ITEM

Communicate your plans. Share garden updates regularly to keep everyone informed. Ask your school administrator to help your team plan a groundbreaking or dedication ceremony. They may also assist by sharing the event with local media and district officials. Set the date:

☐ START SMALL & DREAM BIG

Thriving, vibrant gardens are inviting and breed success. Weedy, neglected gardens give school gardening a bad name. Remember to dream big but start small until you are sure the entire community is committed to this project. Touch base regularly with your initial stakeholder group to assess what is working and what may need attention.

1. Host a brainstorming session to kickstart your school garden program.

⇛ ACTION ITEM

Write down important ideas here:

----

2. Invite stakeholders, including students, parents, teachers, administrators, food service staff, grounds maintenance staff, and community partners, to share their big ideas. Be sure to include your local county extension agents in this meeting.[1]

3. Use this process to dream big and without judgment. Write down every idea; you never know where it will lead.

4. Next, prioritize what you can accomplish now, what you can achieve later, and what may not work for this project. Having a clear set of S.M.A.R.T. (specific, measurable, achievable, relevant, timely) goals for the short and long term is essential.

5. Agree on a starting place and make an action plan.

⇛ ACTION ITEM

List top three action items to begin working on now:

SCAN THE SCHOOLYARD

Where will your garden grow? You do not need a large area to create a bountiful garden. Raised beds can be purchased or built to accommodate nearly any size space. As the school garden team surveys the schoolyard for a garden site, ask these questions:

1. GARDEN ACCESSIBILITY: Does this location provide easy access for the students and educators who will be using the garden? If you and your students must walk more than a few steps from the building, your garden may suffer from neglect. Additionally, an easily visible garden is more secure and highly valued by the community.

2. ACCESS TO WATER: Is there a nearby water access point on the exterior of the building? Remember, food crops should only be irrigated using potable water. Rain barrels work well for supplying irrigation to ornamental gardens, but if you plan to eat from the garden, a municipal water source is recommended for everyone's safety.[2]

3. FULL SUN: Will this location receive full sun most of the day? Vegetables and herbs need a minimum of 6 hours of sunlight to flourish.

4. GOOD DRAINAGE: Does the area flood? Is the location in the path of stormwater as it flows to a storm drain? Do downspouts discharge near the area? Observe the school grounds during heavy rain. Watch how the water moves off the eaves or roofline of the building and across the site. Stormwater runoff from roofs and paved areas can be polluted, carrying a variety of contaminates. Never place gardens in the path of runoff or near storm drains.[3]

5. STORAGE: Plan for storage solutions for tools, gloves, supplies, and the watering hose. A hose reel will help keep the watering hose from being damaged during mowing.

Don't forget to involve students in the site selection process!

⟫ ACTION ITEM

1. Draw the school grounds and mark where you think the garden should go. Be sure to include the school, parking lots, playgrounds, sport fields, and any potential hazards.

2. Identify 1-3 possible locations for your garden and discuss each with the team and school administration to decide which is best.

3. Sketch or indicate where future garden expansion will be located.

☐ LEARN THE ROPES

Clemson Extension's training program *School Gardening for S.C. Educators* provides online training. Clemson Extension agents are available to provide technical support. Together, we are here to give educators the support and knowledge needed to grow vegetables in raised bed gardens confidently. Topics covered in training include:

1. Planning the Garden
2. Raised Bed Gardening Basics
3. Crop Plans & Seasonality
4. Food & Garden Safety
5. Pest Management
6. Community & Volunteer Resource Development

The South Carolina Department of Education has approved renewal credits for licensed educators. Check with the instructor for more details.

This seasonal planting guide and calendar offers a visual layout and quick reference for suitable crops to plant, common issues, and a harvesting guide.

☐ USING THE OUTDOOR CLASSROOM

School Gardening for S.C. Educators offers K-8 curricula for garden-based learning aligned with South Carolina education standards. *The Garden STEM (Science, Technology, Engineering, and Math)* is a K-8 curriculum[4] packed with lessons you can use in your garden classroom. Please encourage students to get their hands dirty at every opportunity. Work with your garden team to develop opportunities for your students to participate in hands-on learning as often as possible!

> Now that you have built a team, jump to page 10 to learn about important technical information you'll need to grow. vegetables in SC!

COMMUNITY GARDEN
CHECKLIST & WORKSHEET

Community gardens connect neighbors, co-workers, and families in neighborhoods, community centers, churches, workplaces, schools, and food banks. They may ease financial strains on family food budgets. In areas known as 'food deserts,' community gardens can improve access to fresh produce.

Community gardening provides a safe, recreational activity where people of all ages and abilities can participate. Community gardens allow neighborhoods to share resources such as tools, equipment, and land. Beautification of vacant lots and contributing to a cleaner, greener environment are also vital community gardening outcomes.

The forms community gardens take can be as diverse as the groups they serve. Some community gardens subdivide the land into plots, and others cultivate one large garden shared by many. Some gardens donate all of their harvests to people in need, while others let gardeners keep what they grow to feed their own families; some are a hybrid of the two.

While every garden is as different as the people who work in it, there are vital steps to take before planting the first seed. Use this checklist and worksheet to guide your community garden to success:

☐ 1. HOLD A LISTENING SESSION

Before you jump into a community gardening project, invite at least ten interested stakeholders to a community garden meeting. The first meeting should be a listening session to allow participants to share their concerns, interests, and expectations. Community gardens are labor-intensive and require a team to be successful. Take careful notes so you can gather the input into a cohesive description of the proposed community garden.

List your initial team members here:

☐ 2. FORMALIZE YOUR GROUP

Some community gardeners find that forming garden clubs, adopting by-laws, electing officers, and creating committees are important steps to keep the project focused and energize participants. While this level of organization may seem unnecessary at the onset of your project, as the community garden grows, having structure for future growth aids in sustainability.

Initially, a garden club should have a minimum of two officers, a president, and a treasurer. Creating a garden club will help members feel engaged in establishing the new garden. The garden club board of director's roles typically include:

- Establishing rules of conduct and etiquette;
- Accepting and reviewing garden applications;
- Assigning plots or raised beds to gardeners;
- Collecting annual dues from gardeners (if applicable);
- Paying bills such as rent, water, insurance;
- Resolving conflict or disputes.

☐ 3. CONSIDER THE CHALLENGES AHEAD

Community gardens will inevitably face challenges; discuss plans for dealing with these common issues with gardeners and organizers before you begin.

- **MANAGEMENT & MAINTENANCE:** Create systems to enforce rules and resolve conflicts now to avoid future issues. Consider who will mow the grass? Who will manage fire ants and other pests? Who will repair and maintain equipment?

- **PARTICIPATION:** How will the group maintain a sense of community as interest levels change and leaders come and go?

- **THEFT AND VANDALISM:** Who will coordinate security measures? Communicating with local community leaders, law enforcement, and neighbors can raise awareness of the project.

- **BUILDING GARDENING SKILLS:** Engage with gardening experts such as Extension agents, Master Gardener volunteers, and local garden centers to find classes and training to build gardening skills among gardeners.

- **SUPPLIES & LOGISTICS:** Who will source materials such as soil, compost, lumber, etc.?

- **SUSTAINABILITY:** Leasing or borrowing land means gardens may need to move abruptly. This instability can cause gardens to fail. How will the group handle this should the landowner terminate the use agreement?

- **COMMUNICATION:** Regular meetings to determine planting plans and future growth will keep your community garden growing.

4. LOOK FOR LAND: DOES THE PROPOSED SITE HAVE WHAT IT TAKES?

- ❏ Food safety is a major concern. Before selecting a site read page 22 to learn more about land use history, flooding, and wildlife dangers.

- ❏ Does the site receive full sun? Vegetable gardens need at least 6-8 hours of full sun. Visit the site throughout the day and even different seasons to see if trees or other structures shade the area.

- ❏ Is there a potable water source? A well or municipal water is critical for garden success and food safety. Collected rainwater may not be safe for edible crops; use rain barrels to irrigate non-edible plants such as flowers for pollinators or wash tools and equipment.

- ❏ What is the proximity to the gardeners who will cultivate the garden? If the garden is too far away, gardeners will lose interest.

- ❏ Does your group have permission to use the site? A use agreement or lease should be obtained in writing. A formal lease agreement should be executed to protect all parties involved.

5. DESIGN & INFRASTRUCTURE

- ❏ Make a map to scale, marking important features on the site. Keep copies in a binder and computer files for future reference. Consider accessibility when locating garden beds and other elements of the garden. Design with future growth in mind, such as using care when establishing trees, fences, or other permanent structures.

- ❏ Determine if garden plots will be raised beds or tilled in-ground gardens. Avoid the use of topsoil in raised beds. Amend cultivated in-ground gardens according to soil test results.

- ❏ Determine how you will irrigate garden beds or plots. Drip irrigation reduces plant diseases, diminishes foodborne pathogen concerns, and conserves water.

- ❏ Fences can curb vandalism and deter animal pests. Drive-through gates make accessing garden sites easier for gardeners and equipment.

- ❏ Create a community area with benches, picnic tables, shade, and a storage shed. A simple chalkboard or whiteboard inside the door can be an important communication tool. Consider incorporating additional elements such as a compost area, signage, fruit trees and vines, and perimeter landscaping with herbs or pollinator plants.

Creative planning of community garden spaces can lead to bountiful harvests in unexpected places. Snipes, Z. Clemson University

Now that you have built a team, read on to learn about important technical information you'll need to grow vegetables in SC!

GARDENING GUIDE

RAISED BED GARDENING

School and community gardens are often situated on vacant lots, grassy areas around schools, or underutilized community sites, none of which are particularly ideal for vegetable gardening. Challenges such as compacted soil, poorly drained soils, and large volumes of weed seeds lurking beneath the soil surface can be exacerbated by tilling up these areas.

There may be plenty of space to till up a new garden, but without mechanized or chemical weed control methods, school and community gardens can quickly become weedy and unsightly.

Raised beds may be constructed of a vast array of materials limited only by the gardener's creativity, aesthetics, and budget. Due to safety concerns, using treated lumber, landscape timbers, and recycled plastic composite lumber are not recommended for school gardens. Creosote-soaked railroad ties and rubber tires should never be used.

Untreated cedar typically lasts between 5 to 7 years in our hot southern climate, making it a safe choice for wooden raised beds. If you choose to build your own raised beds, make sure no nails, screws, or other hardware will threaten gardener safety.

Raised beds may be built to any length but should be no more than 2 to 4 feet wide for gardeners to reach into the center of the beds. Keeping everything within arm's reach helps prevent soil compaction caused by stepping into the beds. Typically, raised beds are 6 to 8 feet long so that gardeners do not have to walk too far to access both sides of the bed.

Paths between beds should be 2 to 4 feet wide or as wide as necessary to accommodate one to two students and or a walker or wheelchair. Wide paths also allow space for wheelbarrows or garden carts to maneuver through the garden. Mulch the walkways to minimize the need for mowing and trimming weeds around raised beds.

Construct or purchase raised beds that are at least 12 to 18 inches deep. Building deeper raised beds that hold more soil will initially cost more. You will need more building materials and soil to fill the beds, but the garden will require less irrigation and, plants will be more productive with less water stress.

Topsoil may introduce weed seeds, soil-borne pathogens, and create soil fertility issues, therefore, it is not recommended. Raised beds are essentially large containers, so it is acceptable to use a soilless growing media. These may be purchased bagged or in bulk. Common blends found on the market contain ground pine bark, sand or vermiculite, limestone, slow-release fertilizer, and compost. Weeds, diseases, fertility, and drainage issues can be reduced using soil-free media. Avoid using peat-based potting soil that can dry out quickly. Avoid the temptation to fill beds with low-cost compost. Plants may thrive for one or two seasons in straight compost, but nutrients are lost rapidly and won't provide long-term support for a healthy garden.

SHEET COMPOSTING

Sheet composting, also known as "lasagna gardening," is a passive composting method in which carbon and nitrogen-rich materials are layered and composted on site. The idea is that you build soils up rather than digging or tilling amendments into the ground. Sheet composting also introduces soil organisms that, through their feeding activities, will begin mixing the native soil with the organic matter above. You will soon start to notice earthworms and other organisms in the soil you've created through sheet composting.

Begin with a cardboard layer directly on the ground under raised beds to smother weeds and encourage microbial soil activity. Add layers of carbon and nitrogen-rich sources inside the raised bed. Begin by putting pats of alfalfa hay down first, then 1 to 2 inches of compost, followed by nitrogen-rich fruit and vegetable scraps, another layer of compost, rotted leaves, more compost, and finally bagged garden soil on top. Moisten each layer well before proceeding and plant in the final layer. Raised bed garden soil should be replenished regularly. Fertilize vegetable gardens with the nutrients they need during the growing season by applying a water-soluble or granular fertilizer at the rate recommended by the manufacturer or based on a soil test report; repeat applications every two to three weeks during the growing season. Do not apply more than the recommended rate of any fertilizer. Overfertilizing can cause plant damage or death.

LAYERS OF A "LASAGNA GARDEN"

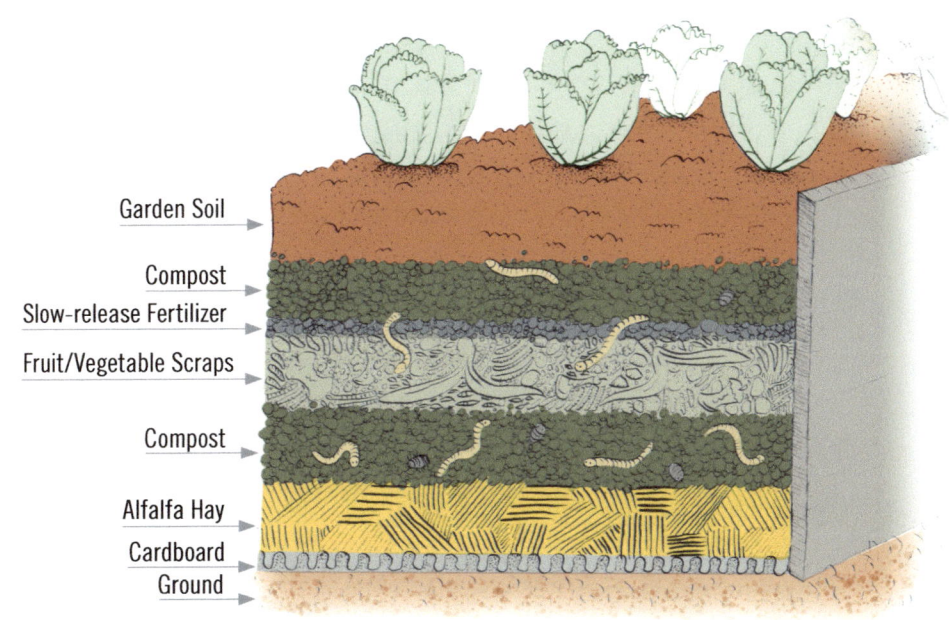

WATERING

Water is essential for growing vegetables, and gardeners must plan to provide supplemental irrigation throughout the year. The most critical times in a plant's life in the garden are the first few weeks after planting and during the development of fruit, roots, or tubers.

Drip irrigation is a system of tubes and emitters that conserves water and minimizes plant diseases. Because leaves are kept dry, and water is delivered at the soil line, less evaporation occurs. Less water splashing on plants also reduces the movement of food-borne pathogens. Overhead sprinklers, watering cans, or hand watering with a hose-end sprayer may exacerbate these concerns and use more water than drip irrigation.

Drip irrigation delivers consistent moisture because emitters used to deliver water are pressure regulated, which means they will not release water until the entire line is pressurized. By contrast, soaker hoses are not pressure regulated, which means water may not be applied evenly. One end of the bed may be soaked while the other end remains dry.

Irrigation frequency and duration vary depending on the type of crop, plant size, temperature, and other environmental factors. Soil should be kept moist and not be allowed to dry out or become saturated. Monitor soil moisture closely, particularly in the warmer months.

SEASONAL CLASSIFICATION OF VEGETABLE CROPS

Seasonal classification of vegetable crops or "seasonality" refers to the window of time when a crop should be planted and harvested.

South Carolina has a long growing season, which means that many vegetables can be grown year-round. Establishing vegetable plants in the garden at the right time of year can maximize school and community gardens' productivity. Planting in the correct season may also reduce insects and diseases, reduce watering needs, and produce more flavorful fruits and vegetables. Crops are divided into two seasonal groups: warm-season and cool-season crops. Warm-season crops are planted once the threat of freezing weather has passed in the spring. Warm-season crops may also be planted in late summer so

they can be harvested before winter temperatures drop. Cool-season crops grow best when air and soil temperatures are cooler, usually in the early spring and mid-late fall. Timing can be tricky because, in South Carolina, early spring may start as early as January or February![5]

COOL-SEASON CROPS		WARM-SEASON CROPS	
HARDY	HALF HARDY	TENDER	VERY TENDER
Broccoli	Beet	Green/Snap Beans	Squash
Collards	Carrot	Eggplant	Sweet Potato
Cabbage	Swiss Chard		Tomato
Kale	Lettuce		Pepper
Onion / Garlic	Kohlrabi		Cucumber
English Pea	Arugula		Okra
Radish	Irish Potato		

Table 1: The United States Department of Agriculture determines plant hardiness zones based on average annual extreme minimum temperatures in a specific geographic location. Hardiness can also refer to a plant's ability to survive the heat or other adverse growing conditions. In this publication, hardiness refers to survival during extreme cold.

When crops are grown in the appropriate season, they will grow faster, use less fertilizer, and water, have fewer pest issues, and yield more than if they were grown out of season. The planting guide, on page 25 can be used to grow crops with seasonality in mind. Learning about common plant families (or at least the plant family members) will help gardeners use their best judgment when deciding when to plant.

PLANT FAMILIES

Crops of the same plant family will often be similar in planting date, have common cultural practices such as fertility and water requirements, and share common pest issues. For example, crops in the Brassica or Cole crop family include collards, kale, broccoli, and cabbage. These crops have very similar planting dates and will experience similar insect and disease issues.

CROP FAMILIES	EXAMPLES
Brassicaceae (sometimes referred to as cole crops)	Broccoli, Collards, Kale, Cabbage, Arugula, Turnip, Radish, Kohlrabi
Cucurbitaceae	Cucumber, Squash, Zucchini, Watermelon, Cantaloupe, Winter Squash (butternut, acorn, etc.)
Asteraceae	Lettuce, Sunflowers
Amaranthaceae (sometimes referred to as goosefoot crops)	Beets, Swiss Chard, Spinach
Solanaceae (sometimes referred to as nightshade crops)	Tomato, Pepper, Eggplant, Irish Potato
Convolvulaceae (sometimes refered to as morning glory)	Sweet Potato
Amaryllidaceae (sometimes referred to as allium family)	Onion, Garlic, Chives, Shallots
Leguminosae	Beans, Peas
Apiaceae	Carrots, Dill, Parsley
Malvaceae	Okra

Learning crop families and their members will also help with crop rotation. Crop rotation is the most important pest management and overall plant health tool that a gardener has. If the same crop or crops of the same family are planted in the same spot year after year, problems will arise. In the planting plan, crop rotation has been built-in. It is imperative that beds are labeled so that rotational plans can be followed. Numbering the beds can be an elaborate art project or it can be as simple as a notation on a piece of paper. An example of crop rotation can be seen in Bed 1 in the planting guide (pages 27-30). Four crops and four crop families are rotated through in one calendar year; squash, onion, English peas and sweet potatoes. By rotating different families, insect pests and diseases cannot build up their populations and the soil remains healthy.

When designing a garden planting plan, it is important to schedule out both planting and harvesting dates. The more planning that goes into the planting and harvesting dates, the higher chances are for success. Remember that in school and community gardens the goal is to have as many gardening days as possible throughout the year while keeping crop rotation and seasonality in mind. The crops chosen for the planting plan are relatively easy to grow, have quick maturity dates, have less pest issues, come from different crop families, and are seasonally appropriate for maximum use of the garden beds.

There are many crops that do well in South Carolina that are not highlighted in the planting guide because they do not fit the criteria mentioned above. Once gardeners have a feel for seasonality, crop rotation, maturity dates, how to plant, and how to properly plan a garden on paper, some crops that would do well include strawberries, potatoes, turnips, rutabagas, mustard greens, cabbage, spinach, leeks, garlic, kohlrabi, basil, cilantro, cucumber, eggplant (fall), and pepper (fall).

On page 34 of this publication, there are plan rotations you can follow.

FRUIT IN THE GARDEN

Most fruit is grown on perennial plants, which means it may take several years to enjoy a harvest. While many fruit varieties can be grown in South Carolina, school and community gardeners need to make appropriate selections for their garden site. Fruit trees are generally not recommended for school gardens because the fruit typically reaches maturity during the summer months when students are not present. Some fruit trees are more challenging to maintain than others, requiring chemical pest and disease control to yield fruit. Fortunately, there are many easier to grow options for school and community gardeners to grow.

Blueberries, figs, muscadines, blackberries, and pears are productive with relatively low inputs and are easy to integrate into the garden landscape. In contrast, apples, peaches, nectarines, plums, and nut trees are challenging to grow in the South without regular pesticide applications.

Perennial fruit crops require careful attention to location, soil preparation, and variety selection. Always purchase fruit trees, shrubs, and vines from a reputable nursery or mail-order company.

School and community gardeners should do extensive research and consult their county extension agents before selecting and planting.

Annual fruits such as watermelon, cantaloupe, and honeydew melons are widely grown by farmers in South Carolina, but these crops are not ideal for school gardens. Their sprawling growth habit, high disease occurrence, pest pressures, and summer harvest time make them difficult to grow. Community gardeners should plan carefully so these crops do not overtake other gardeners' plots.

Strawberries are an excellent choice for school gardeners as they are harvested during the school year and are ideal for growing in small gardens. Strawberries are also fun to incorporate into edible landscapes.

In South Carolina, strawberries grow best using the annual hill system, which takes advantage of South Carolina's mild winters. In this system, strawberry plants are planted in the fall, typically October, allowed to overwinter in the garden, and harvested in the spring. Each plant is then terminated or removed from the garden by June. Strawberries planted in spring do not yield as many berries. Gardeners should note that it can be challenging to find strawberry plants in the fall.

Strawberries are a sweet garden treat in early to mid-spring. Snipes, Z. Clemson University

HERBS IN THE GARDEN

Herbs make useful and versatile additions to any garden. Culinary herbs such as mint, rosemary, and thyme are perfect for snipping into recipes and are easy to grow. Most herbs grow best in well-drained soil and full sun.

Nectar sipping hummingbirds, butterflies, and bees are attracted to flowering herbs. The tiny flowers of many common herbs also attract beneficial insects such as small wasps and flies that help to control insect pests on nearby vegetables. Herbs such as dill, parsley, and fennel provide larval host food for swallowtail butterflies.

Herbs such as rosemary, marjoram, lemon balm, and mint can become downright aggressive in the rich soil found in raised bed gardens. Plant perennial herbs in separate containers or in their own beds or borders to prevent them from overtaking the vegetable garden. Interplant annual herbs such as basil, dill, and cilantro and leave some to flower in the garden to attract pollinators and other beneficial insects.

Herbs such as lemon thyme, add flavor to meals and interest to the garden. Dabbs, A. Clemson University

RECOMMENDED HERBS FOR SCHOOL AND COMMUNITY GARDENS		
NAME	**WHEN & HOW TO ESTABLISH**	**HOW TO USE IT**
Basil (*Ocimum basilicum*)	Warm-season annual. Seed or transplant. Full sun.	Fresh leaves used in pesto, salads and pizza. May be preserved by dehydrating or frozen chopped in oil.
Chives (*Allium schoenoprasum*)	Hardy perennial. Seed or transplant. Full sun.	Cut fresh or dehydrated. Flowers are edible.
Cilantro (*Coriandrum sativum*)	Cool-season annual. Seed or transplant. Full to part sun.	Chopped fresh leaves used in salsa and other dishes; seeds are known as coriander used pastries and other baked goods.
Dill (*Anethum graveolens*)	Cool-season annual. Seed or transplant. Full sun.	Fresh leaves used to season fish and eggs; seeds and flowers used for pickling or garnishes.
Parsley (*Petroselinum crispum*)	Hardy biennial. Seed or transplant. Full to part sun.	Fresh leaves used as garnish or in salads.
Rosemary (*Salvia rosmarinus*)	Hardy perennial. Transplant. Full sun.	Fresh leaves, dehydrated.
Thyme (*Thymus species*)	Hardy perennial. Transplant. Full sun.	Fresh leaves, dehydrated.

MANAGING PESTS IN SCHOOL & COMMUNITY GARDENS

"If you build it, they will come" can have several meanings in the garden. Inevitably insects and diseases will become commonplace in gardens. Insects and plant diseases can provide engaging learning opportunities for gardeners of all ages. When pests do arrive in the garden, integrated pest management (IPM)[6] techniques should be employed to manage them. IPM is a way to manage pests in the least toxic manner and involves cultural control, mechanical control, biological control, and lastly chemical control.

There are a few steps involved in the IPM process:

1. Frequent the garden area as much as possible and take note of the insects present.

2. Correctly identify the pest; remember that not all bugs are pests (See chart "Common Pests of Vegetables" page 22).

3. Determine the number of pests that will be detrimental to the health or aesthetics of the plant.

4. Decide on a management technique.

Below are lists of cultural, mechanical, biological, and chemical controls used in IPM. How many of these are you using in your garden?

CULTURAL CONTROL

- ❑ Select the proper location for the plant; right plant, right place;

- ❑ Maintain good soil fertility and proper moisture management;

- ❑ Plant at the correct time;

- ❑ Grow resistant or tolerant varieties;

- ❑ Keep weeds out of the garden and surrounding area; they harbor insects and diseases;

- ❑ Proper planting depth and spacing between plants;

- ❑ Use healthy, robust transplants and good quality seed;

- ❑ Rotate crops from season to season;

- ❑ Stake and trellis tall crops;

- ❑ Prevent injury to plants.

MECHANICAL CONTROL

- Hand pick any diseased leaves, insect pests, or weeds;

- Install insect netting and other physical barriers;

- Use organic mulches such as straw, cardboard, bark, or hay to suppress weeds around gardens.

BIOLOGICAL CONTROL

- Support the native beneficial insect populations by having flowering plants year-round that attract and provide food and shelter;

- Conserve native insect populations by avoiding the use of broad spectrum insecticides (for example products that contain the following active ingredients: carbaryl, malathion, chlorpyrifos, bifenthrin, or imidacloprid).

CHEMICAL CONTROL

NOTE: Chemical controls are a last resort in any IPM plan. They should be used only on an as-needed basis when all other avenues of pest control have been explored. In order to apply pesticides (even organic-approved) to school gardens and some community gardens, you must have the appropriate pesticide license. It is against the law to apply pesticides on a property that you do not own without the proper license. Pesticides purchased at stores as well as homemade remedies are considered pesticides and cannot be applied to school gardens without the appropriate license. For more information on pesticide regulations see Clemson University Department of Pesticide Regulation.[7]

- Always read and follow the label directions. It is a violation of federal law to use a pesticide product in a manner inconsistent with its labeling.

- Use the least toxic product first,

- Spray late in the evening to prevent harm to bees and other beneficial insects.

> See pages 20 & 21 for a list of diseases and insects gardeners are likely to encounter in the garden.

POLLINATORS & BENEFICIAL INSECTS

Only a small percentage of insects are considered plant pests. Still, they have the potential to cause a significant amount of damage in gardens. The overwhelming majority of insects are considered beneficial and are welcome in the garden. There are approximately 26,350 species of beneficial insects in North America.

Insect species from many different families serve as plant pollinators. They provide critical pollination services that allow fruits, vegetables, and flowers to complete their life cycles. Without these pollinating insects, crops such as squash and watermelons would never develop their delicious fruits.

Some insects are considered beneficial because they act as predators and parasitoids, preying on pests in the garden. Predators such as praying mantids, ladybird beetles, dragonflies, and assassin bugs actively hunt or ambush their prey. Parasitoids use other insects to complete their life cycles. Tachinid fly females lay their eggs in soft-bodied tomato hornworm caterpillars. The larvae emerge, consuming the internal portion of the caterpillar. This process ultimately kills the destructive caterpillar and introduces many more beneficial insects into the garden all without chemical controls.

Pest populations can often be kept in balance by predators or parasitoids so that gardeners do not need to intervene. The best way to support beneficial insects is to plant more flowers! Diverse habitats support more insect diversity. Some flowers to consider adding to your garden beds include:

- Buckwheat (*Fagopyrum esculentum* 'Mancun' or 'Lifago')
- Zinnias (*Zinnia elegans* 'Cut and Come Again')
- French marigolds (*Tagetes patula*)
- Sweet alyssum (*Lobularia maritima*)
- Cosmos (*Cosmos bipinnatus*)
- Allow herbs such as cilantro, dill, and basil to flower.
- Leave a few brassica family crops to go to flower at the end of the season, such as arugula, collards, or broccoli.[24]

A variety of flowers supports beneficial insect populations. *Snipes, Z. Clemson University*

How many species of beneficials can you identify in your garden?

Tiny parasitoid wasps and flies deposit their eggs inside their hosts' bodies. Their larvae develop within, killing the host.

Adult syrphid flies feed on nectar and pollen of flowers. Their larvae feed voraciously on soft-bodied insects like aphids, thrips, and whiteflies.

Assassin bugs hide in and around crops and flowers to stalk their prey. They use their straw-like mouthparts, or proboscis, to suck the nutrients out of their prey.

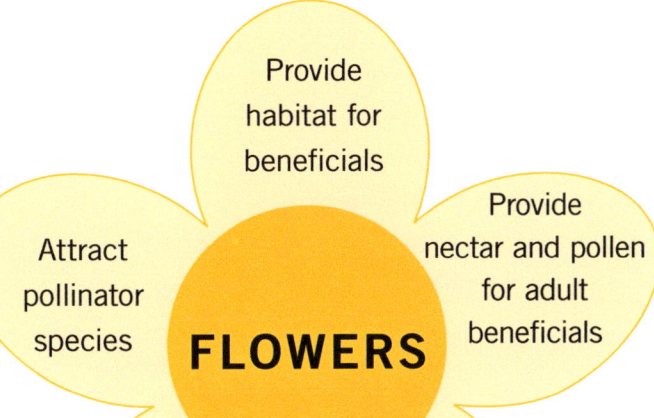

FLOWERS
- Provide habitat for beneficials
- Attract pollinator species
- Provide nectar and pollen for adult beneficials
- Add aesthetic appeal to the garden
- Can be grown year-round

Many species of wasps actively hunt caterpillars that feed on vegetables

Native bees are attracted to flowers and can provide pollination services to crops in the garden.

Adult and immature ladybird beetles feed on aphids, a common garden pest. Ladybird beetles are welcome predators in the garden.

Parasitoids are insects that develop within their host

An aphid mummy is all that is left after an aphid is parasitized by a tiny beneficial wasp.

This leaffooted bug has two tiny white eggs of the Tachnid fly laid on it. The eggs will hatch and bore into its body.

The white projections coming from this caterpillar are cocoons of a parasitic wasp.

COMMON PESTS OF VEGETABLE CROPS

CROPS	LEPIDOPTERAN INSECT PESTS (CATERPILLARS)	COLEOPTERAN PESTS (BEETLES)	HEMIPTERAN PESTS (TRUE BUGS)	OTHER PESTS
Collards, Kale, Cabbage, Kohlrabi Broccoli, Arugula, Radish [8]	cabbage looper, diamondback moth, cabbage webworm, cross-striped cabbageworm, imported cabbageworm	yellow-margined leaf beetle, flea beetles	harlequin bug, cabbage aphid, turnip aphid, whiteflies	grasshoppers
Squash & Zucchini, Cucumber [9]	melon worm, pickleworm, squash vine borer	cucumber beetle (spotted, striped, banded), squash beetles	melon aphid, squash bug, leaf-footed bug, stink bugs (many species),whiteflies	nematodes, two-spotted spider mite
Beets & Swiss Chard [10]	cutworms, armyworm, cabbage looper, diamondback moth	flea beetles	aphids	nematodes
Sweet Potato [11]	armyworms (many species)	wireworm complex (potato wireworm, tobacco wireworm), cucumber beetle, flea beetles, grubs (May and June beetles), sweet potato weevil	potato leafhopper	Transporting sweet potatoes is restricted in some counties in South Carolina due to quarantine for the sweet potato weevil (*Cyals formicarius*). Please check with the Clemson University Department of Plant Industry for guidance.
Tomato[12], Irish Potato, Pepper[13], Eggplant [14]	hornworm, tomato fruit worm	Colorado potato beetle	potato aphid, stink bug (many species), leaffooted bug	nematodes, two-spotted spider mite, thrips
Peas & Beans [15]	lesser cornstalk borer, cabbage borer, corn earworm	Mexican bean beetle, cowpea curculio	aphids (many species), stink bugs (many species), tarnished plant bug	thrips, two-spotted spider mite

COMMON DISEASES OF VEGETABLE CROPS					
CROPS	DISEASES CAUSED BY FUNGI	DISEASES CAUSED BY WATER MOLDS	DISEASES CAUSED BY BACTERIA	DISEASES CAUSED BY VIRUSES
Collards, Kale, Cabbage, Kohlrabi, Broccoli, Arugula, Radish [16]	Alternaria leaf spot, wirestem, Sclerotinia stem rot, Fusarium yellows	damping off, downy mildew	black rot, soft rot, bacterial blight	Cucumber mosaic (CMV)
Squash & Zucchini, Cucumber [17]	powdery mildew, gummy stem blight, Alternaria leaf spot, anthracnose, Fusarium wilt	downy mildew, phytophthora	Bacterial wilt	Cucumber mosaic (CMV), Watermelon mosaic (WMV)
Beets & Swiss Chard [18]	Cercospora leaf spot, damping off	Downy mildew	(no major diseases)	(no major diseases)
Sweet Potato [19]	scurf, black rot, Fusarium wilt	pythium damping off	(no major diseases)	(no major diseases)
Tomato [20], Irish Potato, Pepper [21], Eggplant [22]	early blight, southern blight, Fusarium wilt, Verticillium wilt, Anthracnose fruit rot	late blight	bacterial wilt, bacterial spot, bacterial soft rot	Tomato spotted wilt (TSWV), Tobacco mosaic (TMV), others
Peas & Beans [23]	Anthracnose, root rots (Rhizoctonia, Fusarium), rust, powdery mildew, Cercospora leaf spot, white mold	root rot	bacterial blights	mosaic viruses

FOOD SAFETY, HARVESTING, AND STORAGE [25]

The most critical thing school and community gardeners should focus on is food safety. Farmers keep our nation's food supply safe by using Good Agricultural Practices (GAP); from the field to the market and our tables, everyone along the supply chain maintains records and documentation. School and community gardens can also ensure a safe food supply by employing some of these same GAP principles.

Every school or community garden should keep records outlining the garden's location, potential food safety risks, emergency, and standard operating procedures. This book's appendix offers reproducible templates of logs and checklists to document your food safety activities.

GAP certification is a process that a farm or garden may pursue through the South Carolina Department of Agriculture. This certification process has a fee associated with it and requires annual auditing. Only school or community gardens that plan to sell the produce they grow to a school are required to be GAP certified. You do not need to be GAP certified to donate produce, sell it through a market or farm stand or give it away to students or community gardeners.

Although everyone may not need to be certified, applying GAP principles to any garden program will make the food supply safer and more secure.

For more information on GAP plans, certification, and food safety procedures, please contact your local Clemson Extension Agent. [26]

BEFORE ESTABLISHING A GARDENING SITE

Research the history of the land you intend to use. Former landfills, dumping grounds, and industrial sites could pose significant food safety risks to gardeners by leaving behind dangerous contaminants in the soil, air, and water. Clemson Extension does not recommend gardening activities on these sites, often designated brownfields by the U.S. Environmental Protection Agency (EPA). The EPA defines a brownfield as "a property, the expansion, redevelopment, or reuse of which may be complicated by the presence or potential presence of a hazardous substance, pollutant, or contaminant."[27] Before moving forward with any gardening project, investigate land-use history by researching online records that may indicate past land use. For more guidance, see the EPA Brownfields and Urban Agriculture: Interim Guidelines for Safe Gardening Practices publication.

Excessive rainwater runoff and flooding is a major concern when growing food crops. Water carries pathogens that can cause illness in humans. Before choosing a garden site, observe the area during a rain event to note where excess rainwater flows. Observe roof eaves, drainage grates, and parking lots to see if the water is moving over the proposed site. If the garden area floods, any produce growing there must be destroyed. Therefore, select a different garden site before this situation arises.

Garbage bins, dumpsters, and chemical storage sheds may contaminate produce or attract wildlife. Locate gardens away from any potential contamination sources, preferably uphill from these sites.

Wildlife is more than a nuisance; animals visiting gardens may introduce food-borne pathogens by feeding, defecating, and trampling the garden. Locate gardens away from wildlife habitat, erect barriers such as fences or netting, secure seeds, compost bins, and other potential food sources. Never place birdhouses or birdfeeders near or in gardens where food is growing.

DURING THE GROWING AND HARVESTING SEASON

- Workers must be trained on food safety and procedures specific to the garden (standard operating procedures);
- Hand washing is a critical component of food safety and should be done frequently;
- Stay out of the garden if you are sick;
- Report any injuries or sickness to the person responsible for food safety;
- Do not harvest crops that have come into contact with urine, feces, or blood;
- Keep animals away from gardens and monitor for animal activity and feces in the garden and harvest areas;
- DO NOT use manure;
- Water should be monitored for pathogens (municipal water is best for food safety). Do not use collected rainwater on edible crops;
- Harvest bins, scissors, clippers, knives must be kept clean and sanitized;
- Produce should be washed and properly stored (see table on page 24).

See pages 54-58 for reproducible food safety templates for record keeping.

HARVESTING & STORING PRODUCE

CROPS	PREPARATION AFTER HARVEST	STORAGE REQUIREMENTS FOR OPTIMAL SHELF LIFE	SHELF LIFE AT OPTIMAL CONDITIONS
Lettuce, Arugula	Refrigerate and wash before use	32 F	21 days
Collards, Kale, Chard	Refrigerate and wash before use	32-36 F	1-3 weeks
Broccoli, Cabbage	Refrigerate and wash before use	32-36 F	Broccoli-1-2 weeks, Cabbage 2-4 months
Squash and Zucchini	Refrigerate and wash before use	41-50 F	2 weeks
Beets, Carrots, Radish	Wash, dry, refrigerate	32-36 F	3-5 months
Dried Onion	Allow to cure in sun for a few days, wipe soil off, wash before use	Cool, dark, humidity controlled environment (pantry, closet)	4-6 months
Green or Spring Onion	Refrigerate and wash before use	32 F	7-10 days
Green Beans and Peas	Refrigerate and wash before use	37-45 F	5-10 days
Sweet Potatoes	Cure sweet potatoes by digging and storing at 80-85 F and 85-90% humidity for 10 days. Wipe off dried soil once cured. Wash before use.	Once cured, store in a cool (55-60 F), dark location.	6 months or more

24

SCHOOL & COMMUNITY GARDENS
PLANTING GUIDE

The next section offers a recommended school garden planting plan and calendar. Although this plan follows a school calendar, community gardeners may also find this plan beneficial if their gardeners will take long vacations or cannot work in the heat of summer.

This plan's key features include seasonal diagrams for raised bed gardens that include spacing recommendations and method of establishment for each crop. The accompanying calendar illustrates planting and harvesting windows and offers a notes section at the right of the calendar pages.

Gardeners ready to expand to year-round gardening may use the provided planning worksheet and sample planting plans for a seasonally appropriate year-round garden with more variety.

Before you begin, locate your county on the map. All planting plans in this publication will refer to dates that correlate with Piedmont or Coastal Plain.

PIEDMONT
Abbeville | Anderson | Cherokee | Chester | Chesterfield | Edgefield | Fairfield | Greenville | Greenwood | Lancaster | Laurens | McCormick | Newberry | Oconee | Pickens | Saluda | Spartanburg | Union | York

COASTAL PLAIN
Aiken | Allendale | Bamberg | Barnwell | Beaufort | Berkeley | Calhoun | Charleston | Clarendon | Colleton | Darlington | Dillon | Dorchester | Florence | Georgetown | Hampton | Horry | Jasper | Kershaw | Lee | Lexington | Marion | Marlboro | Orangeburg | Richland | Sumter | Williamsburg

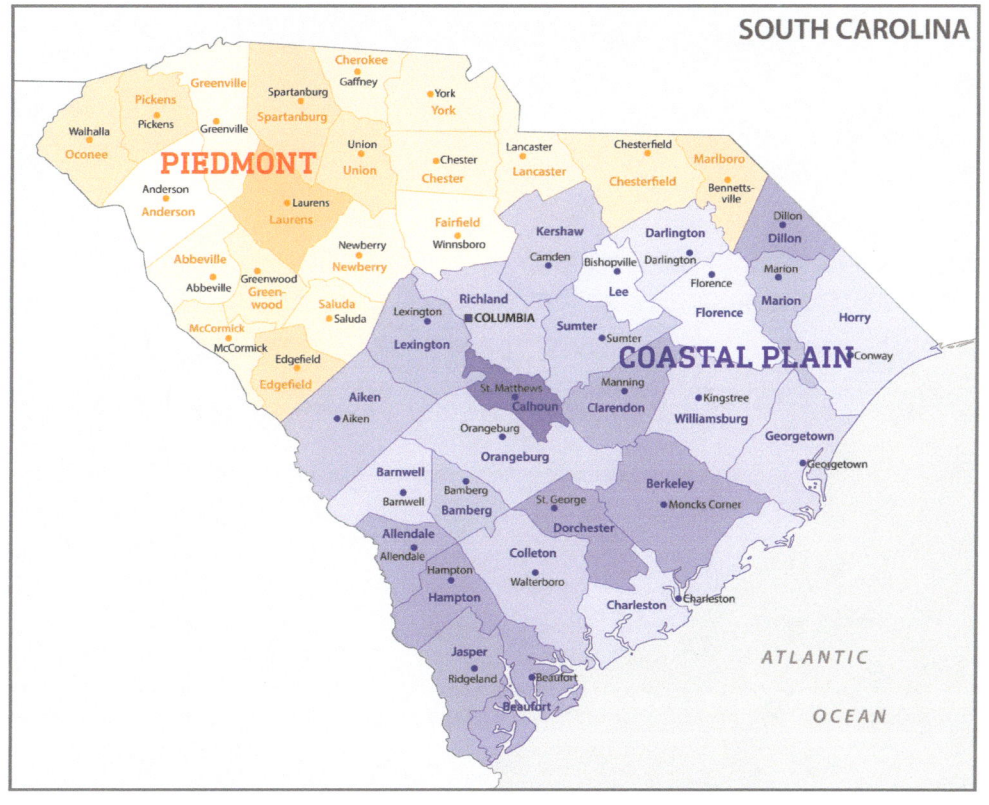

RECOMMENDED PLANTING PLAN AND CALENDAR FOR SCHOOL GARDENS

PLANTING PLAN

The planting guide section illustrates a recommended school garden design comprised of four raised beds connected in a long rectangle. Removing spaces between raised beds reduces maintenance issues and allows more area for gardening. Each bed is four feet wide by four feet long, allowing children to reach into the center of the bed. Creating mulched paths or an apron around a set of beds reduces maintenance and creates clear, safe pathways for young gardeners to easily navigate. For more recommendations about raised bed gardening, refer to page 10.

It is essential to label the four beds numerically (1-4) in your garden so that you can manage the recommended planting plan properly. Creating labels for raised beds could become a fun art project for students.

Through each season of the school year, you will grow crops from unrelated plant families in the numbered beds. This crop rotation is one way to reduce disease and insect issues in your garden.

Each numbered bed uses illustrations to show which crop to plant, how the crop should be established, (i.e., from seed or transplant), and how to space the crop relative to the other plants or seeds.

Each page is labeled by the season in the garden based on the school calendar. The year-round growing season in South Carolina means we can produce a wide variety of vegetables in our gardens.

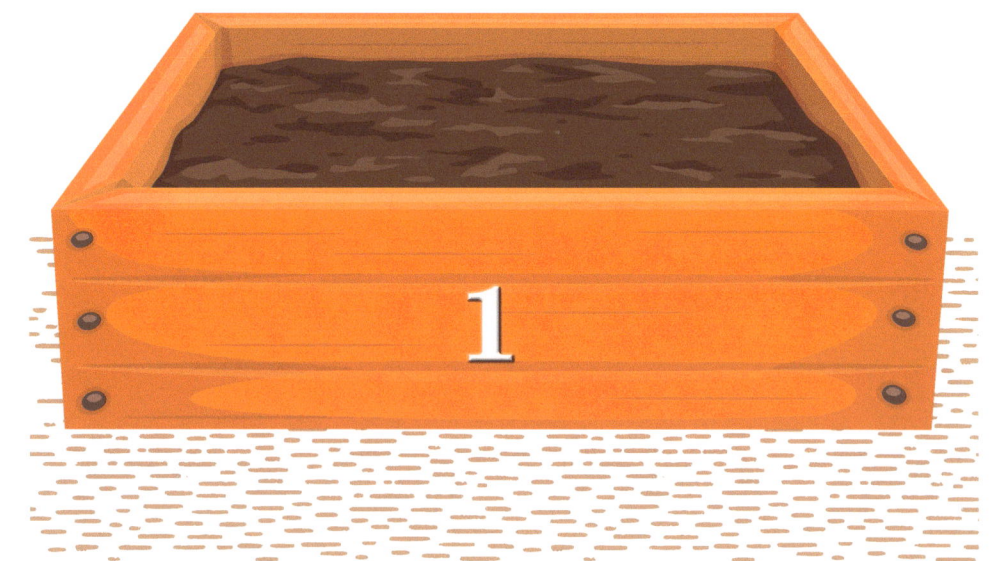

26

EARLY FALL PLANTING PLAN (AUG-OCT)

CROP NAME	SQUASH #1	SNAP/GREEN BEANS #2	CARROTS & BEETS #3	BROCCOLI #4
PLANT FROM	Seed	Seed	Seed	Transplant
PLANT SPACING	30 inches	5 inches	Sprinkle seeds evenly across bed and thin to 2 inches between plants at 14 days.	12 inches
ROW SPACING	24 inches	30 inches		36 inches
PLANTING DEPTH	1.5 inches	1-1.5 inches	0.5-0.75 inches	Plant root ball so that the top is even with the soil line in the bed.
TOTAL PLANTS	5-6	18-20		8
SPECIAL NOTES	Plant two seeds in each hole and thin to one plant using scissors after ten days.	Plant two seeds in each hole and thin to one plant using scissors after ten days.	Divide the bed in half. Plant one half with carrot seeds and one half with beet seeds.	

LATE FALL PLANTING PLAN (NOV-DEC)

CROP NAME	ONIONS #1	KALE #2	ONIONS #3	BROCCOLI #4
PLANT FROM	Bulb	Transplants	Bulb	Still growing from early fall
PLANT SPACING	2 inches	16 inches	2 inches	
ROW SPACING	12 inches	10 inches	12 inches	
PLANTING DEPTH	1-2 inches Gently push bulbs into soil until pointed end is facing up and 1-2" below soil line.	Plant root ball so that the top is even with the soil line in the bed.	1-2 inches	
TOTAL PLANTS	90-100	12	90-100	
SPECIAL NOTES	Periodically harvest every other onion in the row so other onions can grow larger.	Space cabbage 18 inches apart if kale is unavailable.	Periodically harvest every other onion in the row so other onions can grow larger.	

EARLY SPRING PLANTING PLAN (JAN-MARCH)

CROP NAME	ENGLISH PEAS #1	LETTUCE #2	ONIONS #3	COLLARDS #4
PLANT FROM	Seed	Transplants	Still growing from late fall	Transplants
PLANT SPACING	3 inches	12 inches		16 inches
ROW SPACING	16 inches	16 inches		10 inches
PLANTING DEPTH	1 inch	Plant root ball so that the top is even with the soil line in the bed.		Plant root ball so that the top is even with the soil line in the bed.
TOTAL PLANTS	45-55	12		12
SPECIAL NOTES	Trellis each row for easier picking.	Lettuce seeds need light to germinate. Scatter seeds evenly across soil surface. Press lightly to make sure seeds are in contact with soil. Harvest using clean scissors at desired size.		

LATE SPRING PLANTING PLAN (MARCH-MAY)

CROP NAME	ENGLISH PEAS #1	LETTUCE #2	RADISH #3	COLLARDS #4
PLANT FROM	Still growing from early spring	Still growing from early spring	Seed	Still growing from early spring
PLANT SPACING			Sprinkle seeds evenly across bed and thin to 2 inches between plants at 14 days.	
ROW SPACING				
PLANTING DEPTH			.5 inches	
TOTAL PLANTS				
SPECIAL NOTES				

SUMMER PLANTING PLAN (JUNE-JULY)

CROP NAME	SWEET POTATOES #1-4
PLANT FROM	Transplants
PLANT SPACING	12 inches
ROW SPACING	24 inches
PLANTING DEPTH	Plant root ball so that the top is even with the soil line in the bed.
TOTAL PLANTS	6 per bed
SPECIAL NOTES	

RECOMMENDED SCHOOL GARDEN CALENDAR
AUGUST

MONDAY	TUESDAY	WEDNESDAY	THURSDAY	FRIDAY	SATURDAY	SUNDAY	TO DO:

THIS WEEK:
1 2 Harvest Sweet Potatoes from summer

THIS WEEK:
1 Plant Squash
2 Plant Green Beans

THIS WEEK:
1 Plant Squash
2 Plant Green Beans

KEY

Plant from bulbs =

Plant from seeds =

Plant from transplants =

Bed number =

Time to Harvest =

Time to Prepare =

Piedmont dates in

Coastal Plain dates in

Piedmont & Coastal Plain dates

RECOMMENDED SCHOOL GARDEN CALENDAR
SEPTEMBER

MONDAY	TUESDAY	WEDNESDAY	THURSDAY	FRIDAY	SATURDAY	SUNDAY

THIS WEEK:
- [3] [4] Harvest Sweet Potatoes
- [3] Plant Beets
- [3] Plant Carrots
- [4] Plant Broccoli

TO DO:

KEY
- Plant from bulbs = 🌷
- Plant from seeds = 🌰
- Plant from transplants = 🌱
- Bed number = 🏷️
- Time to Harvest = 🧺
- Time to Prepare = 🧤
- Piedmont dates in ▇ (orange)
- Coastal Plain dates in ▇ (purple)
- Piedmont & Coastal Plain dates ▇ (blue)

RECOMMENDED SCHOOL GARDEN CALENDAR
OCTOBER

MONDAY	TUESDAY	WEDNESDAY	THURSDAY	FRIDAY	SATURDAY	SUNDAY	TO DO:
		THIS WEEK: 1 Get ready for Squash harvest 2 Get ready for Green Bean harvest					

KEY

Plant from bulbs =

Plant from seeds =

Plant from transplants =

Bed number =

Time to Harvest =

Time to Prepare =

Piedmont dates in 🟧

Coastal Plain dates in 🟪

Piedmont & Coastal Plain dates 🟦

RECOMMENDED SCHOOL GARDEN CALENDAR
NOVEMBER

MONDAY	TUESDAY	WEDNESDAY	THURSDAY	FRIDAY	SATURDAY	SUNDAY
		THIS WEEK: Get ready for Beet harvest (Bed 3); Get ready for Broccoli harvest (Bed 4)				
		THIS WEEK: Plant Onions (Bed 1); Plant Kale (Bed 2)				
		THIS WEEK: Harvest Carrots and Beets (Bed 3); Plant Onions (Bed 3)				

TO DO:

KEY
- Plant from bulbs
- Plant from seeds
- Plant from transplants
- Bed number
- Time to Harvest
- Time to Prepare
- Piedmont dates in orange
- Coastal Plain dates in purple
- Piedmont & Coastal Plain dates in blue

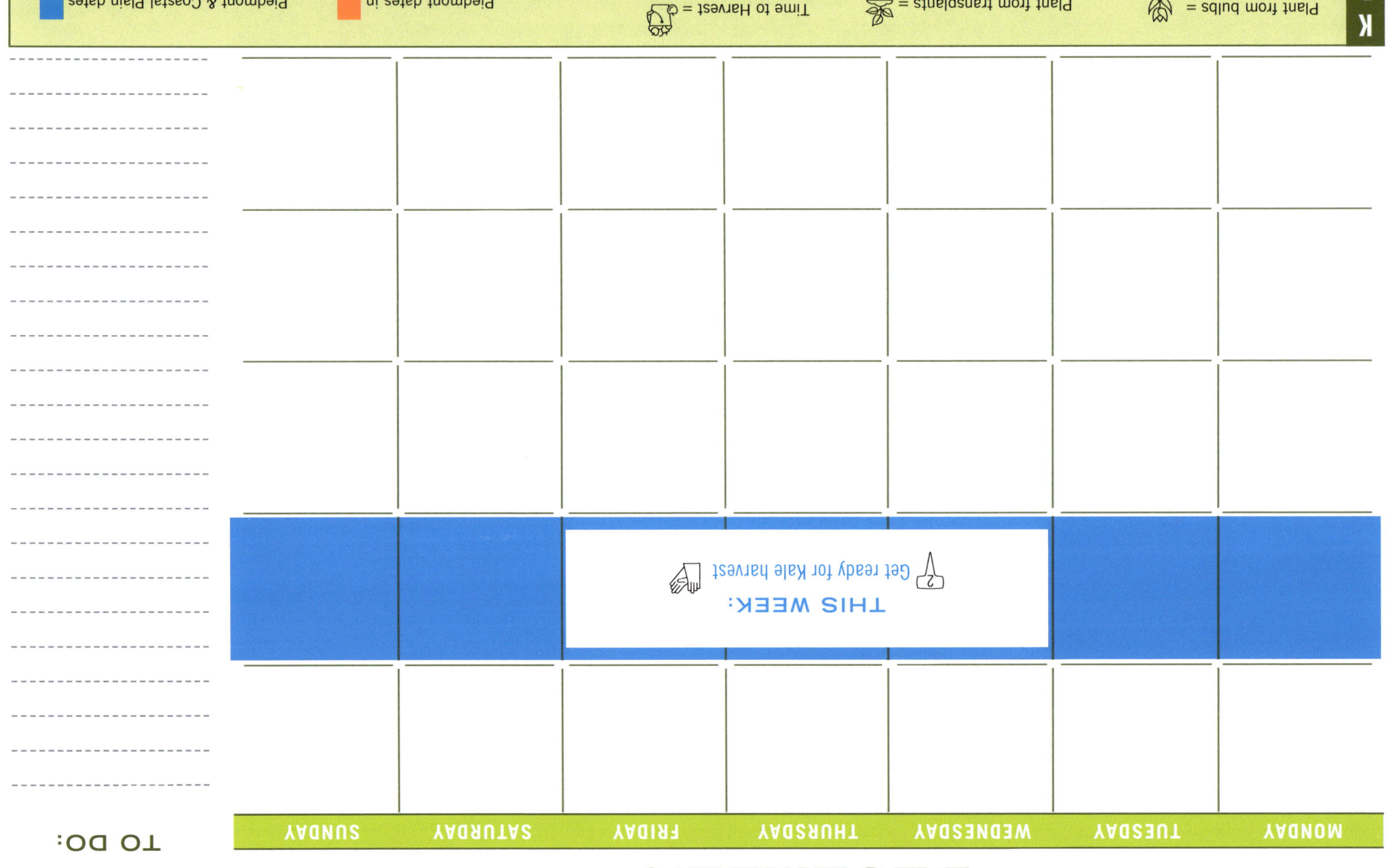

RECOMMENDED SCHOOL GARDEN CALENDAR
JANUARY

MONDAY	TUESDAY	WEDNESDAY	THURSDAY	FRIDAY	SATURDAY	SUNDAY

THIS WEEK:
- [Bed 2] Continue harvesting Kale
- [Bed 4] Continue harvesting Broccoli

TO DO:

KEY
- Plant from bulbs =
- Plant from seeds =
- Plant from transplants =
- Bed number =
- Time to Harvest =
- Time to Prepare =
- Piedmont dates in (orange)
- Coastal Plain dates in (purple)
- Piedmont & Coastal Plain dates (blue)

RECOMMENDED SCHOOL GARDEN CALENDAR
FEBRUARY

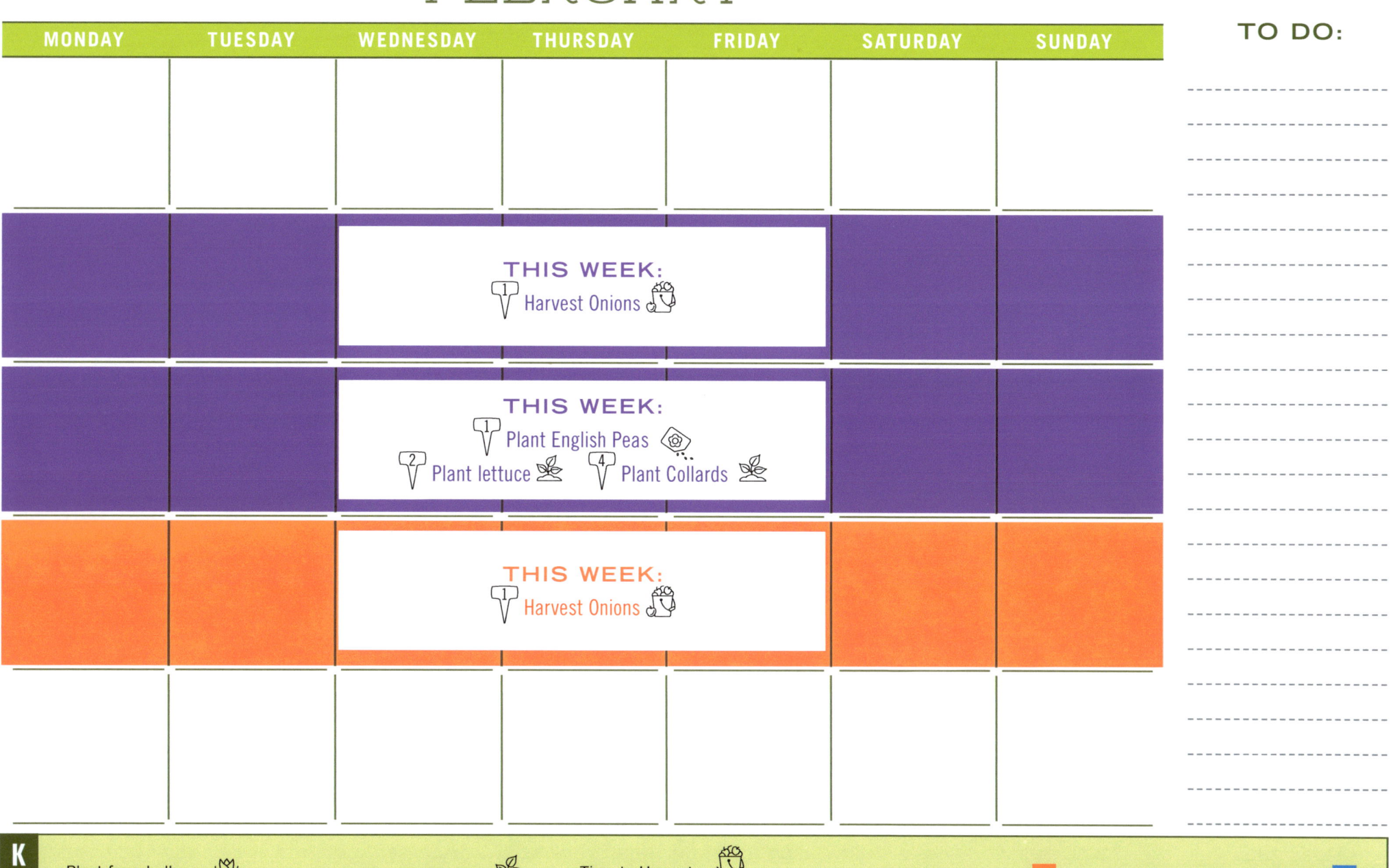

MONDAY	TUESDAY	WEDNESDAY	THURSDAY	FRIDAY	SATURDAY	SUNDAY

THIS WEEK:
1 Harvest Onions

THIS WEEK:
1 Plant English Peas
2 Plant lettuce   4 Plant Collards

THIS WEEK:
1 Harvest Onions

TO DO:

KEY

Plant from bulbs =

Plant from seeds =

Plant from transplants =

Bed number =

Time to Harvest =

Time to Prepare =

Piedmont dates in

Coastal Plain dates in

Piedmont & Coastal Plain dates

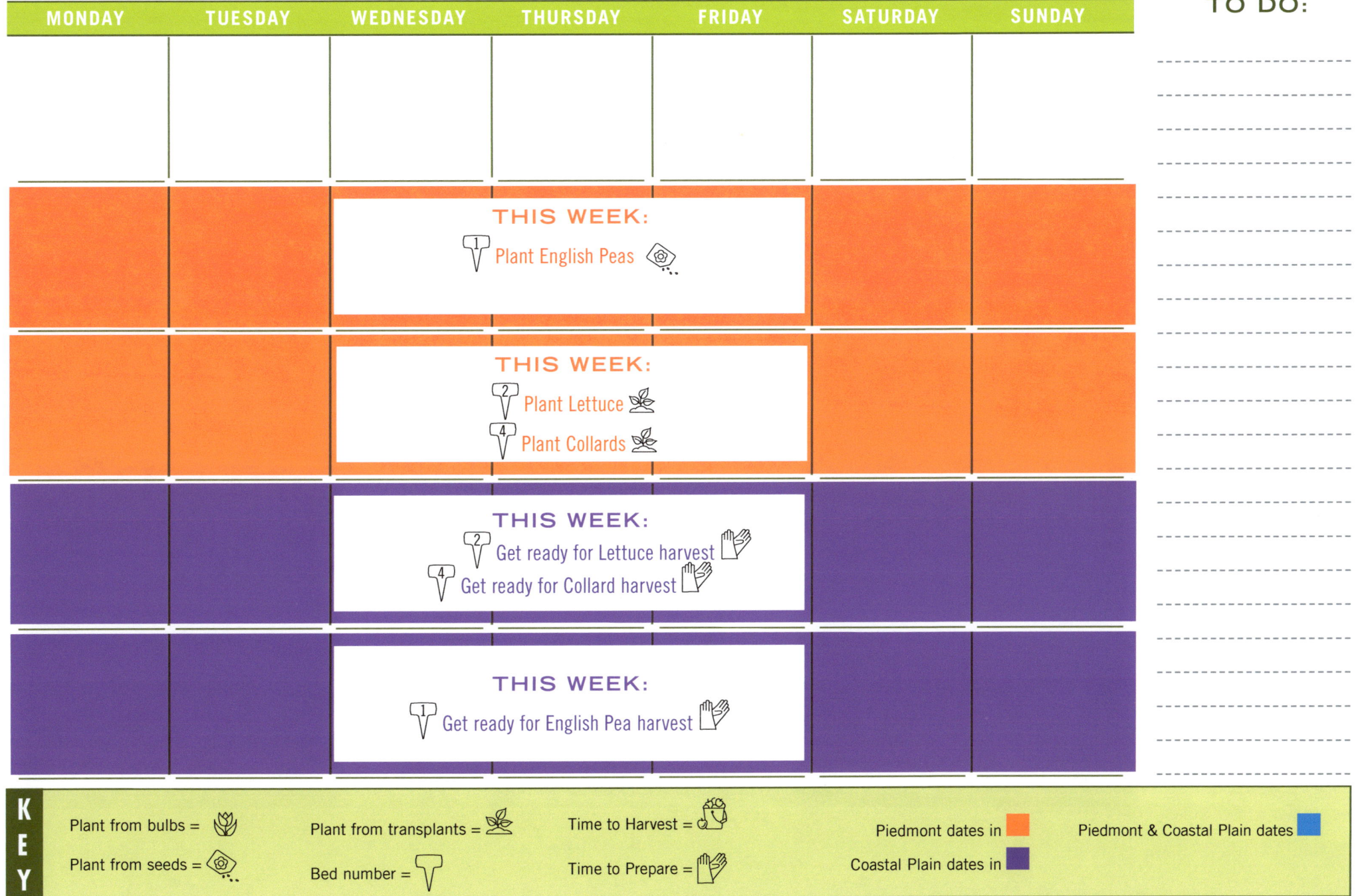

RECOMMENDED SCHOOL GARDEN CALENDAR
APRIL

MONDAY	TUESDAY	WEDNESDAY	THURSDAY	FRIDAY	SATURDAY	SUNDAY	TO DO:

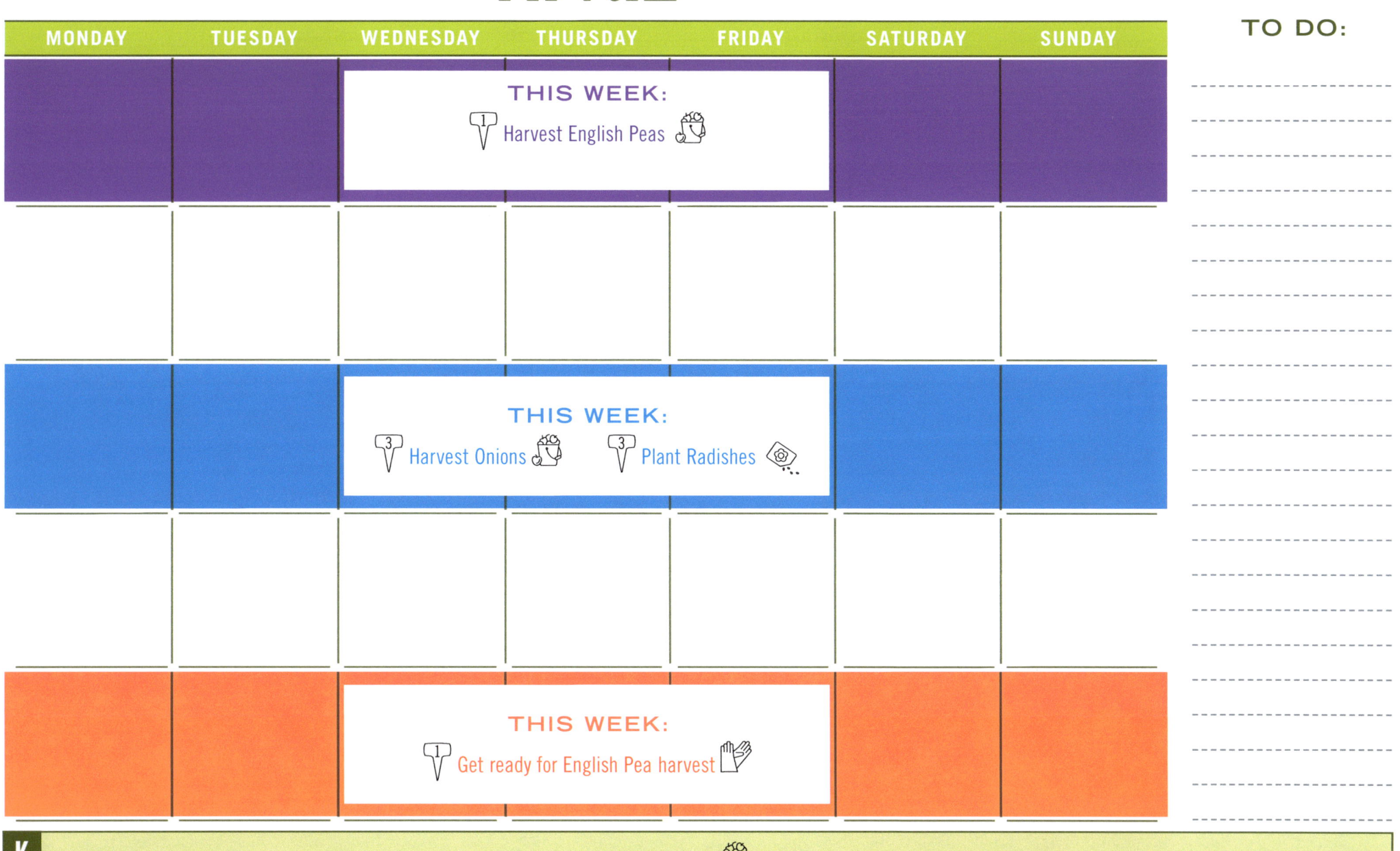

THIS WEEK:
1 Harvest English Peas

THIS WEEK:
3 Harvest Onions   3 Plant Radishes

THIS WEEK:
1 Get ready for English Pea harvest

KEY

Plant from bulbs =
Plant from seeds =
Plant from transplants =
Bed number =
Time to Harvest =
Time to Prepare =
Piedmont dates in (orange)
Coastal Plain dates in (purple)
Piedmont & Coastal Plain dates (blue)

RECOMMENDED SCHOOL GARDEN CALENDAR
MAY

MONDAY	TUESDAY	WEDNESDAY	THURSDAY	FRIDAY	SATURDAY	SUNDAY

THIS WEEK: (Piedmont)
- Bed 2: Get ready for Lettuce harvest
- Bed 4: Get ready for Collard harvest

THIS WEEK: (Piedmont & Coastal Plain)
- Bed 4: Harvest all Collards
- Bed 3: Harvest Radishes
- Beds 1, 2, 3, 4: Plant Sweet Potatoes

TO DO:

KEY
- Plant from bulbs
- Plant from seeds
- Plant from transplants
- Bed number
- Time to Harvest
- Time to Prepare
- Piedmont dates in (orange)
- Coastal Plain dates in (purple)
- Piedmont & Coastal Plain dates (blue)

PLANNING A YEAR-ROUND SCHOOL OR COMMUNITY GARDEN

Crop planning is an essential tool that allows gardeners to maximize the number of growing days in a season. Crop planning can also help gardeners implement crop rotations, an integral part of pest management. Planning a year-round garden while juggling planting dates and crop rotations can be challenging. We have taken the guesswork out of the process by providing nine pre-designed crop plans in the following pages.

Each plan contains a variety of crops to span the entire growing season. Use this step-by-step guide and worksheet to choose and implement a planting plan incorporating your garden favorites.

1. Review the nine pre-designed crop plans outlined on page 44 and note which rotation will produce the vegetables you like to eat and fit your garden space. Make a note of your favorite crop plan(s) here: e.g., Plan 2, Plan 7, Plan 9, etc.:

- -

2. Use a copy of your community garden base map or sketch your raised bed(s) or garden row(s) on a piece of graph paper.

3. Each crop rotation plan represents a physical location in the garden (bed, row, or pot) and spans one full calendar year. Label the raised bed(s) or row(s) on your map with the crop rotation plan you will follow this year in that physical space.

Assign one crop plan to each bed or row OR repeat the same rotation plan for multiple garden spaces. For example, Plan 1 could be repeated in multiple beds, rows or pots.

4. Remember that to reap the maximum benefit from the pre-designed crop rotation, do not deviate from the crops listed, and be sure to plant in the season outlined. If you must make substitutions, be sure to select plants from the same plant family with similar days to maturity, for example, substituting collards for kale or cabbage.

5. Finally, research recommended varieties and determine specific planting dates for your region using factsheets from the Clemson Extension Home & Garden Information Center website.[28] The plans provided here only describe when crops will be growing; further research will be needed to determine exact planting or seeding dates. Many variables such as weather, soil temperature, and transplant availability can alter a crop's planting dates. In some cases, these circumstances may mean there is not enough time to grow and harvest a suggested crop. It is acceptable to skip a crop within the crop plan and leave the garden spot empty until planting the next crop. For maximum, year-round garden yields, plant or seed recommended crops immediately after harvesting the previous one. Page 43 offers a pictorial example of a year-long crop rotation using the pre-designed Plan 1.

TIMELINE OF A YEAR-ROUND CROP PLAN
(EXAMPLE PLAN 1)

Plan 1 offers an example of the window of time crops will be growing throughout the calendar year in the same physical location.

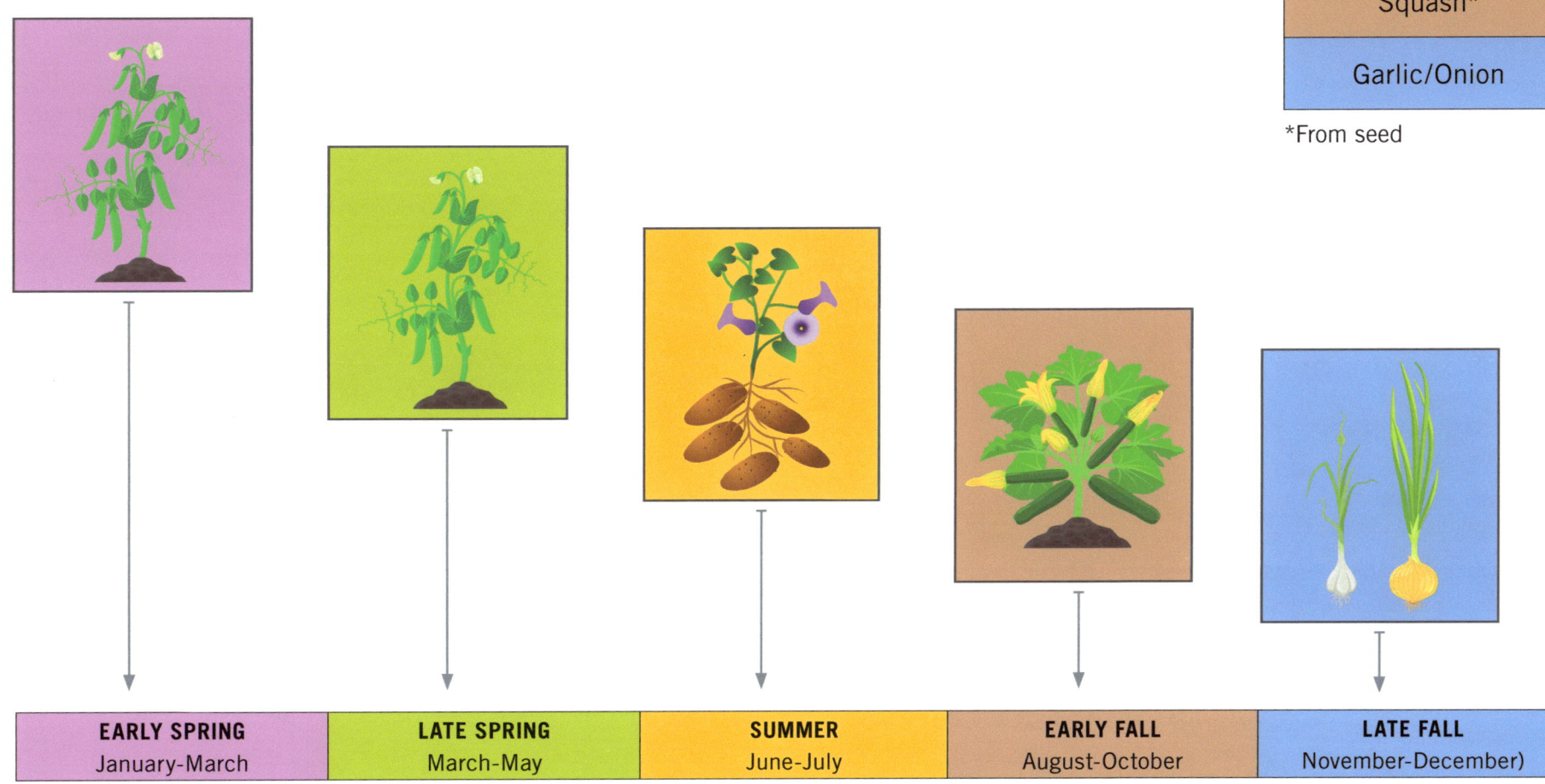

PLAN 1
English Peas*
English Peas*
Sweet Potato
Squash*
Garlic/Onion

*From seed

EARLY SPRING	LATE SPRING	SUMMER	EARLY FALL	LATE FALL
January-March	March-May	June-July	August-October	November-December)

CROP PROFILES
SCHOOL & COMMUNITY GARDENS

CROP	PREFERRED METHOD OF PLANTING & SPACING*	DATES TO PLANT	APPROXIMATE DAYS TO HARVEST	HARVESTING TIPS	GARDENERS NOTES
PLANT FAMILY: BRASSICACEAE					
Cabbage [29]	Transplant 6-8 spaced evenly.	SPRING Piedmont: 3/15-4/30 Coastal Plain: 2/1-3/31 FALL Piedmont: 7/15-8/30 Coastal Plain: 8/15-9/30	75-85 Days (depending on variety)	Cut entire head with knife or sharp shears just above the soil line. Remove outer leaves prior to storage in refrigerator.	Research and experiment with the wide variety of cabbage types available such as storage, flat, pointed, red, savoy and Napa.
Collards [30]	Transplant 9-12 spaced evenly.	SPRING Piedmont: 3/15-6/30 Coastal Plain: 2/1-6/15 FALL Piedmont: 8/1-9/30 Coastal Plain: 8/1-10/30	28 Days to harvest lower leaves 70 Days to harvest entire plant	Use shears or break off leaves at the bottom first. Leave 6-8 of the newest leaves at the top so the plant will continue to grow and can be harvested over several months, or wait until mature to harvest entire plant at soil line.	Collards are South Carolina's state vegetable. South Carolina is second in collard green production in the nation.
Kale [31]	Transplant 9-12 spaced evenly.	SPRING Piedmont: 2/1-6/15 Coastal Plain: 3/15-6/30 FALL Piedmont: 8/1-10/30 Coastal Plain: 8/1-10/30	28 Days to harvest lower leaves 70 Days to harvest entire plant	Use shears or break off leaves at the bottom first. Leave 6-8 of the newest leaves at the top so the plant will continue to grow and can be harvested over several months, or wait until mature to harvest entire plant at soil line.	Tuscan kale also known as dinosaur kale makes great kale chips.

CROP	PREFERRED METHOD OF PLANTING & SPACING	DATES TO PLANT	APPROXIMATE DAYS TO HARVEST	HARVESTING TIPS	GARDENERS NOTES
Broccoli [32]	Transplant 6-8 spaced evenly.	SPRING Piedmont: 3/20-4/30 Coastal Plain: 3/1-4/10 FALL Piedmont: 8/15-9/15 Coastal Plain: 9/1-9/30	55-85 Days (depending on variety)	Cut the head of the broccoli with garden shears or a knife when it is about 6 inches across, and the beads (flower buds) are still tight. Cutting the main stem will encourage smaller side shoots to produce. These can be harvested for weeks after the main head is harvested.	The beads or florets of broccoli are unopened flower buds. If left unharvested, the flowers will bloom. Beneficial insects and pollinators love the flowers of broccoli. Broccoli flowers are edible!
Arugula [33]	Sow seeds evenly over surface and lightly press into soil.	SPRING Piedmont: 2/1-6/15 Coastal Plain: 3/15-6/30 FALL Piedmont: 8/1-9/30 Coastal Plain: 8/1-9/15	30-40 Days	Harvest arugula with scissors or garden shears at any size you prefer. Arugula can be harvested three or more times, about a week or so apart.	Like broccoli, arugula flowers are also edible and attract beneficial insects.
Radishes, [34] salad or garden type	Sow evenly over surface and thin with scissors to 2' apart to allow root formation.	SPRING Piedmont: 2/1-6/15 Coastal Plain: 3/15-6/30 FALL Piedmont: 8/1-9/30 Coastal Plani: 8/1-9/15	25 Days	Harvest radishes by pulling them by hand.	Keep radishes well-watered so they do not become hot and tough to eat.
PLANT FAMILY: CUCURBITACEAE					
Summer Squash & Zucchini [35]	Sow two seeds in 5 equally spaced holes. Thin to one plant if both germinate. Use scissors to cut the extra seedling. Do not pull.	SPRING Piedmont: 4/15-7/30 Coastal Plain: 4/1-5/30 FALL Piedmont: 8/1-9/30 Coastal Plain: 8/1-9/15	50 Days	Harvest when fruit are small and shiny every 2 days or sooner. Harvest with sharp scissors or pruners to avoid injury to plant. May be harvested over three or more weeks.	Squash needs pollinators for fruit production. Flowers are edible and are great stuffed with cheese.

CROP	PREFERRED METHOD OF PLANTING & SPACING*	DATES TO PLANT	APPROXIMATE DAYS TO	HARVESTING TIPS	GARDENERS NOTES
Cucumber [36]	Bush-type cucumber, plant 2 seeds in three equally spaced holes. Thin to one plant if both seeds germinate. Use scissors to thin. Vine-type cucumber, plant 2 seeds in two equally spaced holes as above.	SPRING Piedmont: 4/15-6/5 Coastal Plain: 3/15-5/15 FALL Piedmont: 8/1-8/30 Coastal Plain: 8/1-8/30	55-70 Days	Harvest when young and tender. Both pickling and slicing type cucumbers can be grown in South Carolina gardens.	Trellising can help when harvesting and saves space in the garden.
PLANT FAMILY: AMARANTHACEAE					
Beet & Swiss Chard [37]	Sow seeds over bed and thin to 2" apart a few weeks after germination.	SPRING Piedmont: 3/15-5/31 Coastal Plain: 2/15-3/31 FALL Piedmont: 7/15-8/31 Coastal Plain: 8/15-9/30	50 Days Beets 28 Days Baby Swiss Chard 55 Days mature Swiss Chard	Beets are ready when the root is 2-4 inches in diameter. Remove entire beet plant by hand to avoid damaging roots. Harvest chard with shears, a few inches above soil line to allow plants to re-grow for multiple harvests.	Beets are grown for their roots, but their greens and stems can be eaten and are often used in stir fries. Swiss chard 'Bright Lights' has rainbow colored stems.
PLANT FAMILY: CONVOLVULACEAE					
Sweet Potato [38]	Transplant using "slips" or transplants. 6 spaced evenly.	SPRING Piedmont: 5/1-6/15 Coastal Plain: 4/15-6/15	90-120 Days small fingerling-size sweet potatoes 120-170 Days baking-size sweet potatoes	Check for desired size and maturity by digging under one plant. To harvest, remove vines and dig sweet potatoes. Allow to cure by laying in the sun for a few days. Store in a cool, dry place for several months.	Slips are rooted vine cuttings. Gardeners can cut tips and root them to propagate their own slips. Leaf and stems can be stir fried throughout the growing season. Compost vines at the end of the season.

CROP	PREFERRED METHOD OF PLANTING & SPACING*	DATES TO PLANT	APPROXIMATE DAYS TO HARVEST	HARVESTING TIPS	GARDENERS NOTES
PLANT FAMILY: SOLANACEAE					
Eggplant [39] **Tomato** [40] **Pepper** [41]	Transplant 2-3 eggplants or tomatos 3-6 peppers. Number of transplants will be based on mature size of variety.	SPRING Piedmont: 5/1-6/30 Coastal Plain: 4/1-4/30 FALL Piedmont: Not recommended Coastal Plain: 8/1-8/31	65-100 Days (depending on variety)	Harvest fruit with pruners or scissors to avoid damaging plants. Regular harvests encourage fruit production. Tomatoes may be harvested early and allowed to mature indoors to avoid insect, disease, or weather damage.	Plan to provide support in the form of trellises or cages for these crops. In the heat of the summer, pepper and eggplants can be ratooned, or cut 6-8 inches above the soil. They will continue growing and produce a fall crop.
Potato [42]	6-8 seed pieces spaced evenly. Plant 3-5 inches deep.	SPRING Piedmont: 3/15-4/30 Coastal Plain: 2/1-3/31.	80-100 Days for fingerling-size potatoes 100-130 Days for baking size potatoes	Allow potato vines to die completely before digging. Leave in the ground a week to toughen up the skin on potatoes.	Plant small whole "seed potatoes" or cut larger seed potatoes into "seed pieces". Each seed piece should weigh at least 2 ounces (approximately the size of a ping pong ball) and have one green "eye" or growth point. Plant seed pieces so that "eyes" face up. The use of rubber tires is not recommended due to food safety concerns.
PLANT FAMILY: LEGUMINOSAE					
English Peas [43]	Plant two rows of seeds 2 feet apart. Place a trellis in the middle of the bed to support plants. Plant seeds 1 inch apart within the rows.	SPRING Piedmont: 3/1-4/15 Coastal Plain: 2/1-3/15 FALL Piedmont: 8/15-10/30 Coastal Plain: 8/15-11/30	55 Days for edible pods 65 Days for shelled peas	Harvest as snap peas when pods are young and tender. Harvest as shelling or English peas when pods are fully developed. Harvest peas with scissors to avoid damaging vines.	Gently tie vines to a trellis to aid in harvest and keep plants off the soil. The tendrils, or curly tips and flowers of peas are edible. Use as garnishes on soups, salads and other dishes.

CROP	PREFERRED METHOD OF PLANTING & SPACING*	DATES TO PLANT	APPROXIMATE DAYS TO HARVEST	HARVESTING TIPS	GARDENERS NOTES
Green/Snap Bean [44]	Plant 2 seeds in 18-20 holes even spaced. Thin smaller seedling with scissors after 10 days.	SPRING Piedmont: 4/15-7/1; Coastal Plain: 4/1-6/1 FALL Piedmont: 7/20-8/1; Coastal Plain: 8/1-9/1	50 Days	Harvest beans when they are young to avoid chewy, stringy beans. Harvest with scissors or pruners to avoid damaging plants. May be harvested 3 or more times per week for up to 3 weeks.	Bush varieties of beans are recommended for small gardens and raised beds. Pole or vine type beans should be supported with trellises and require more space.
PLANT FAMILY: ASTERACEAE					
Lettuce [45]	Seed leaf lettuce over soil surface. Seeds need light to germinate, do not cover. 9-12 head-forming type lettuces; evenly spaced.	SPRING Piedmont: 3/1-5/15 Coastal Plain: 2/1-4/15 FALL Piedmont: Not recommended Coastal Plain: 9/15-11/1	28 Days for leaf lettuce 50 Days for head lettuce	Cut loose leaf lettuce a few inches above the soil line with a sharp pair of scissors for multiple (3-5) harvests throughout the season. Harvest head type lettuce before it becomes pointy at the growing tip.	When a lettuce plant flowers, it is called bolting and the leaves become too bitter to eat. Lettuce flowers are attractive to beneficial insects.
PLANT FAMILY: APIACEAE					
Carrots [46]	Sprinkle seeds evenly across bed and thin to 2 inches between plants after 14 days.	SPRING Piedmont: 2/15-3/31 Coastal Plain: 2/1-3/15 FALL Piedmont: 8/1-9/15; Coastal Plain: 9/1-9/15	70 Days (depending on variety)	Thinning seedlings to 1 to every 2 inches will increase the size of each carrot. Harvest periodically to determine the desired size and time left to maturity.	Pelleted seed, or a protective seed coating, makes for easier planting and better germination. Carrot tops can be used as a savory herb to make carrot top pesto.

CROP	PREFERRED METHOD OF PLANTING & SPACING*	DATES TO PLANT*	APPROXIMATE DAYS TO HARVEST	HARVESTING TIPS	GARDENERS NOTES
PLANT FAMILY: AMARYLLIDACEAE					
Onion [47]	20-30 (or more) bulbs or sets. Gently push bulbs into soil until pointed end is facing up and 1-2" below soil line.	FALL Piedmont: 9/15-10/15 Coastal Plain: 10/1-11/15	30 Days for green or spring onions 100 Days or more for dried onions	Pull green onions by hand. Shake off soil and store in a cool, dry place. Dried onions should be harvested and allowed to dry or cure in the sun for several days.	Plant small dry bulbs, or "sets" which refers to a small onion bulb with green shoots. Sets are often sold without soil, bundled together at nurseries and garden centers.
PLANT FAMILY: ROSACEAE					
Strawberries [48]	9-12 transplants (sometimes called plugs) evenly spaced.	FALL Piedmont: 10/1-10/20 Coastal Plain: 10/15-10/31	Day neutral varieties will flower and produce fruit in the fall and spring. June bearing varieties will produce a heavy crop in the spring. Most strawberry farms in SC have June bearing plants.	Harvest every day to prevent disease and insect issues.	After fruit production ceases, remove entire plants and dispose of them. Managing diseases, weeds, and insect pests for more than one season is very difficult. Plant new plugs or transplants each fall for maximum production.

* Spacing recommendations are based on a 4-foot by 4-foot raised bed.

YEAR-ROUND GARDEN PLANNING CALENDAR

MONTH:

MONDAY	TUESDAY	WEDNESDAY	THURSDAY	FRIDAY	SATURDAY	SUNDAY

TO DO:

KEY

HARVEST LOG [49]

DATE	BED #	PRODUCT HARVESTED	AMOUNT HARVESTED	HARVESTED BY	WHAT DID YOU DO WITH PRODUCE	PRE-HARVEST CHECK FOR ANIMAL PRESENCE	EDUCATOR'S INITIALS
10/2/20	3	Yellow squash	7 squash	Charleston Middle School— Ms. Smith's 2nd period class	Made a squash casserole for 4th period class	No signs of animals or animal feces	JF

HARVEST TOOL AND CONTAINER CLEANING LOG [50]

DATE	WHAT WAS CLEANED?	CLEANED	SANITIZED	COMMENTS/ACTIONS TAKEN	INITIALS
3/1/20	8 Pair of Scissors	X	X	Washed before and after harvest	AP
3/3/20	2 School Gardening Harvest Baskets	X		Taken out of storage, cleaned, used, cleaned, stored	MS
		CLEANED: Washed with soap and water	**SANITIZE:** Treat with chemical to reduce harmful pathogens (e.g., 70% alcohol solution or Quat)		

EMPLOYEE TRAINING LOG [51]

TRAINING TOPIC: PRINT AND CIRCLE THE TRAINING TOPIC

❏ Proper hand washing techniques

❏ Proper harvesting techniques

❏ Proper sanitizing techniques

❏ Garden rules review

❏ Emergency/first aid training pertaining to the garden

❏ Other:

DATE AND TIME:	TRAINER:
LOCATION:	LENGTH OF TRAINING:

TRAINING MATERIAL (PLEASE ATTACH ANY WRITTEN MATERIALS TO THIS LOG WITH A STAPLE):

EMPLOYEE NAME/CLASS (PLEASE PRINT)	EMPLOYEE SIGNATURE
1. *Ms. Bell's First Period Class*	*See attached roster*
2.	
3.	
4.	
5.	
6.	
7.	
8.	
9.	

FIRST AID KIT LOG [52]

Date	Location of First Aid Kit or #	Action: Checked or restocked	If restocked, list added items here	Initials
8/15/20	Office	Checked /stocked	Band aids, ointment, gauze	MP

ILLNESS/INJURY REPORT FORM [53]

(Completed forms will be collected and kept on file by the supervisor)

ILLNESS:

EDUCATOR	DATE	WITNESSES	NAME OF SICK STUDENT/EDUCATOR	TIME OF FIRST SYMPTOMS	SYMPTOMS	SEEK MEDICAL ATTENTION
Mr. Reynolds	2/7/20	Charleston Middle School Garden Club	Johnny Smith	2/7/20- 3rd period; 10:45 AM	Vomiting	Sent to school nurse; not allowed in garden that day

ILLNESS/INJURY REPORT FORM [54]
(Completed forms will be collected and kept on file by the supervisor)

INJURY:

EDUCATOR	DATE	WITNESSES	NAME OF INJURED STUDENT/ EDUCATOR	INJURY REPORTED	INJURY REPORTED TO ADMINISTRATOR AND PARENTS	ACTIONS TAKEN FOR INJURED	ACTIONS TAKEN ON FARM
Ms. Brown	4/15/20	Ms. Brown's 1st period class	Jane Doe	Small cut on left index finger from scissors	Yes/yes	Washed hands, cleaned the wound, dressing applied	Stopped using scissors; cleaned and sanitized them; threw away squash that was contacted

ENDNOTES

1 Find your Clemson Extension county agents here:
https://www.clemson.edu/extension/

2 Morganello, K. C. Rainwater Harvesting Systems Guidance for Schoolyard
Applications. 3 Aug. 2021, from https://hgic.clemson.edu/factsheet/rainwater-
harvesting-systems-guidance-for-schoolyard-applications/

3 Guidance on Safety of Flood-Affected Food Crops. 5 May 2020, from
https://www.fda.gov/regulatory-information/search-fda-guidance-documents/guidance-
industry-evaluating-safety-flood-affected-food-crops-human-consumption

4 Donohoe, K., et al. *The Garden Stem*. The College of Charleston, 2015.

5 Kemble, J. (Ed.). (2021). 2021 Southeastern US Vegetable Crop Handbook.
Retrieved March 12, 2021,
from https://content.ces.ncsu.edu/southeastern-us-vegetable-crop-handbook

6 Bellinger, Robert G., et al. "Integrated Pest Management (IPM)." Home &
Garden Information Center | Clemson University, South Carolina, 12 Aug. 1999,
from hgic.clemson.edu/factsheet/integrated-pest-management-ipm/

7 Clemson University Department of Pesticide Regulations: https://www.clemson.
edu/public/regulatory/pesticide-regulation/licensing/index.html

8 Griffin, R., Williamson, J., & Snipes, Z. (2020, May 04). Cabbage, broccoli &
other cole crop insect pests. Retrieved April 12, 2021,
from https://hgic.clemson.edu/factsheet/cabbage-chinese-cabbage/

9 Griffin, R., Williamson, J., & Snipes, Z. (2020, September 07). Cucumber,
squash, melon & other cucurbit insect pests. Retrieved April 12, 2021, from
https://hgic.clemson.edu/factsheet/cucumber-squash-melon-other-cucurbit-insect-pests/

10 Kluepfel, M., Smith, P., Smith, B., & Williamson, J. (2016, August 21). Carrot,
beet, radish & parsnip. Retrieved April 12, 2021,
from https://hgic.clemson.edu/factsheet/carrot-beet-radish-parsnip/

11 Griffin, R., & Williamson, J. (2019, February 07). Sweet potato & Irish potato
insects. Retrieved May 06, 2021,
from https://hgic.clemson.edu/factsheet/sweet-potato-irish-potato-insects/

12 Griffin, R., Khan, M., & Williamson, J. (2019, November 11). Tomato insect
pests. Retrieved April 12, 2021,
from https://hgic.clemson.edu/factsheet/tomato-insect-pests

13 Dufault, R., Doubrava, N., & Ballew, J. (2020, May 12). Pepper. Retrieved April
12, 2021, from https://hgic.clemson.edu/factsheet/pepper/

14 Ballew, A. (2020, August 25). Eggplant insect pests & diseases. Retrieved April
12, 2021, from https://hgic.clemson.edu/factsheet/eggplant-insect-pests-diseases/

15 Griffin, R., & Williamson, J. (2019, May 06). Bean & southern pPea insect
pests. Retrieved April 12, 2021,
from https://hgic.clemson.edu/factsheet/bean-southern-pea-insect-pests/

16 Doubrava, N., Blake, J., & Williamson, J. (2020, April 30). Cabbage, broccoli &
other cole crop diseases. Retrieved April 12, 2021,
from https://hgic.clemson.edu/factsheet/cabbage-broccoli-other-cole-crop-diseases/

17 Doubrava, N., Blake, J., Keinath, A., & Williamson, J. (2020, January 27).
Cucumber, squash, melon & other cucurbit diseases. Retrieved April 12, 2021,
from https://hgic.clemson.edu/factsheet/cucumber-squash-melon-other-cucurbit-
diseases/

18 Kluepfel, M., Smith, P., Smith, B., & Williamson, J. (2016, August 21). Carrot,
beet, radish & parsnip. Retrieved April 12, 2021,
from https://hgic.clemson.edu/factsheet/carrot-beet-radish-parsnip/

19 Kluepfel, M., Blake, J., Keinath, A., & Williamson, J. (2018, December 13). Irish
& sweet potato diseases. Retrieved April 12, 2021,
from https://hgic.clemson.edu/factsheet/irish-sweet-potato-diseases/

20 Griffin, R., Khan, M., & Williamson, J. (2019, November 11). Tomato insect
pests. Retrieved April 12, 2021,
from https://hgic.clemson.edu/factsheet/tomato-insect-pests

21 Dufault, R., Doubrava, N., & Ballew, J. (2020, May 12). Pepper. Retrieved April 12, 2021, from https://hgic.clemson.edu/factsheet/pepper/

22 Ballew, A. (2020, August 25). Eggplant insect pests & diseases. Retrieved April 12, 2021, from https://hgic.clemson.edu/factsheet/eggplant-insect-pests-diseases/

23 Knight, F., & Tanner, C. (2010, February 26). Garden peas. Retrieved April 12, 2021, from https://hgic.clemson.edu/factsheet/garden-peas/

24 Ballew, A. (2018, January 19). Native pollinators. Retrieved April 12, 2021, from https://hgic.clemson.edu/factsheet/native-pollinators/

25 Implementing farm to School Activities: Food safety. (n.d.). Retrieved April 12, 2021, from https://www.fns.usda.gov/cfs/implementing-farm-school-activities-food-safety

26 Find your Clemson Extension county agent here: https://www.clemson.edu/extension/

27 Overview of EPA'S Brownfields program. (2021, February 05). Retrieved April 12, 2021, from https://www.epa.gov/brownfields/overview-epas-brownfields-program

28 https://www.clemson.edu/extension/

29 Smith, P., Doubrava, N., & Smith, B. (2016, August 21). Cabbage & Chinese cabbage. Retrieved April 12, 2021, from https://hgic.clemson.edu/factsheet/cabbage-chinese-cabbage/

30 Smith, P., Doubrava, N., & Ballew, J. (2020, October 28). Collards. Retrieved April 12, 2021, from https://hgic.clemson.edu/factsheet/collards/

31 Ballew, J., & Turner, S. (2021, March 02). Arugula, kale, mesclun, mustard, and swiss chard. Retrieved April 12, 2021, from https://hgic.clemson.edu/factsheet/arugula-kale-mesclun-mustard-and-swiss-chard/

32 Smith, P., Doubrava, N., & Snipes, Z. (2020, July 02). Broccoli. Retrieved April 12, 2021, from https://hgic.clemson.edu/factsheet/broccoli/

33 Ballew, J., & Turner, S. (2021, March 02). Arugula, kale, mesclun, mustard, and swiss chard. Retrieved April 12, 2021, from https://hgic.clemson.edu/factsheet/arugula-kale-mesclun-mustard-and-swiss-chard/

34 Kluepfel, M., Smith, P., Smith, B., & Williamson, J. (2016, August 21). Carrot, beet, radish & parsnip. Retrieved April 12, 2021, from https://hgic.clemson.edu/factsheet/carrot-beet-radish-parsnip/

35 Polomski, B., Bradshaw, D., Shaughnessy, D., Smith, B., & Williamson, J. (2017, November 23). Summer squash. Retrieved April 12, 2021, from https://hgic.clemson.edu/factsheet/summer-squash/

36 Doubrava, O., Doubrava, N., Dufault, R., & Smith, B. (2018, September 19). Cucumber. Retrieved April 12, 2021, from https://hgic.clemson.edu/factsheet/cucumber/

37 Kluepfel, M., Smith, P., Smith, B., & Williamson, J. (2016, August 21). Carrot, beet, radish & parsnip. Retrieved April 12, 2021, from https://hgic.clemson.edu/factsheet/carrot-beet-radish-parsnip/

38 James, S., Polomski, B., & Williamson, J. (2017, January 23). Sweet potato. Retrieved April 12, 2021, from https://hgic.clemson.edu/factsheet/sweet-potato/

39 Doubrava, N., Miller, G., & Ballew, J. (2020, August 31). Eggplant. Retrieved May 06, 2021, from https://hgic.clemson.edu/factsheet/eggplant/

40 Kluepfel, M., Dufault, R., & Williamson, J. (2012, June 26). Tomato. Retrieved May 06, 2021, from https://hgic.clemson.edu/factsheet/tomato/

41 Dufault, R., Doubrava, N., & Ballew, J. (2020, May 12). Pepper. Retrieved May 06, 2021, from https://hgic.clemson.edu/factsheet/pepper/

42 Polomski, B., Bradshaw, D., Shaughnessy, D., & Williamson, J. (2004, April 23). Potato. Retrieved April 12, 2021, from https://hgic.clemson.edu/factsheet/potato/

43 Knight, F., & Tanner, C. (2010, February 26). Garden peas. Retrieved April 12, 2021, from https://hgic.clemson.edu/factsheet/garden-peas/

44 Polomski, B., Bradshaw, D., Shaughnessy, D., & Smith, B. (2016, August 21). Bush & pole-type snap beans. Retrieved April 12, 2021, from https://hgic.clemson.edu/factsheet/bush-pole-type-snap-beans/

45 Smith, P., Polomski, B., Shaughnessy, D., Smith, B., & Williamson, J. (2017, November 23). Lettuce. Retrieved April 12, 2021, from https://hgic.clemson.edu/factsheet/lettuce/

46 Kluepfel, M., Smith, P., Smith, B., & Williamson, J. (2016, August 21). Carrot, beet, radish & parsnip. Retrieved April 12, 2021, from https://hgic.clemson.edu/factsheet/carrot-beet-radish-parsnip/

47 Russ, K., Polomski, B., Smith, B., & Williamson, J. (2016, December 23). Onion, leek, shallot, & garlic. Retrieved April 12, 2021, from https://hgic.clemson.edu/factsheet/onion-leek-shallot-garlic/

48 Kluepfel, M., Polomski, B., & Last, R. (2020, October 08). Growing strawberries. Retrieved April 12, 2021, from https://hgic.clemson.edu/factsheet/growing-strawberries/

49 LaBorde, L., & Lee Stivers Former Extension Educator. (2021, March 26). Tools for writing a farm food safety plan. Retrieved April 12, 2021, from https://extension.psu.edu/tools-for-writing-a-farm-food-safety-plan

50 LaBorde, L., & Lee Stivers Former Extension Educator. (2021, March 26). Tools for writing a farm food safety plan. Retrieved April 12, 2021, from https://extension.psu.edu/tools-for-writing-a-farm-food-safety-plan

51 LaBorde, L., & Lee Stivers Former Extension Educator. (2021, March 26). Tools for writing a farm food safety plan. Retrieved April 12, 2021, from https://extension.psu.edu/tools-for-writing-a-farm-food-safety-plan

52 LaBorde, L., & Lee Stivers Former Extension Educator. (2021, March 26). Tools for writing a farm food safety plan. Retrieved April 12, 2021, from https://extension.psu.edu/tools-for-writing-a-farm-food-safety-plan

53 LaBorde, L., & Lee Stivers Former Extension Educator. (2021, March 26). Tools for writing a farm food safety plan. Retrieved April 12, 2021, from https://extension.psu.edu/tools-for-writing-a-farm-food-safety-plan

54 LaBorde, L., & Lee Stivers Former Extension Educator. (2021, March 26). Tools for writing a farm food safety plan. Retrieved April 12, 2021, from https://extension.psu.edu/tools-for-writing-a-farm-food-safety-plan